LUTHERANS

I N

ECUMENICAL DIALOGUE

A REAPPRAISAL

EDITED BY

Joseph A. Burgess

Augsburg/Minneapolis

LUTHERANS IN ECUMENICAL DIALOGUE
A Reappraisal

Library of Congress Cataloging-in-Publication Data

Lutherans in ecumenical dialogue : a reappraisal / Joseph A. Burgess,
  editor.
    p. cm.
    Includes bibliographical references.
    ISBN 0-8066-2392-6 (alk. paper)
    1. Lutheran Church—United States—Relations. 2. Christian union
conversations—History—20th century. 3. Lutheran Church—
Doctrines—History—20th century. I. Burgess, Joseph A.
  BX8063.7.A1L885   1990
  284.1—dc20   89-29907
                                                      CIP

Manufactured in the U.S.A.   AF 10-4194

94   93   92   91   90   1   2   3   4   5   6   7   8   9   10

Contents

**Part Three: Ecumenism from the Point of View of Each
Church Body**

Abbreviations

AC	Augsburg Confession
Ap	Apology of the Augsburg Confession
ARCIC	Anglican–Roman Catholic International Commission
BC	*Book of Concord. The Confessions of the Evangelical Lutheran Church* (tr. and ed. T. Tappert; Philadelphia: Fortress, 1959)
BEM	*Baptism, Eucharist and Ministry.* Faith and Order Paper 111
CA	*Confessio Augustana* (Augsburg Confession)
COCU	Consultation on Church Union
ELCA	Evangelical Lutheran Church in America
FC Ep	Formula of Concord. Epitome
FC SD	Formula of Concord. Solid Declaration
IA	*An Invitation to Action. The Lutheran–Reformed Dialogue Series III, 1981–1983* (ed. J. E. Andrews and J. A. Burgess; Philadelphia: Fortress, 1984)
LCUSA	Lutheran Council in the U.S.A.
LED 1	*Lutheran–Episcopal Dialogue. A Progress Report* (Cincinnati: Forward Movement, 1972)
LED 2	*Lutheran–Episcopal Dialogue. Report and Recommendations.* The Report of the Lutheran–Episcopal Dialogue, Second Series, 1976–1980 (Cincinnati: Forward Movement, 1981)
L–RC 1	*The Status of the Nicene Creed as Dogma of the Church* (ed. P. C. Empie and W. W. Baum; New York: U.S.A. National Committee of the LWF; Washington, DC: Bishops' Commission for Ecumenical Affairs, 1965)
L–RC 2	*One Baptism for the Remission of Sins* (ed. P. C. Empie and W. W. Baum; New York: U.S.A. National Committee of the LWF; Washington, DC: Bishops' Commission for Ecumenical Affairs, 1966)

5

L–RC 3   *The Eucharist as Sacrifice* (ed. P. C. Empie and T. A. Murphy; New York: U.S.A. National Committee of the LWF; Washington, DC: Bishops' Committee for Ecumenical and Interreligious Affairs, 1967)

L–RC 4   *Eucharist and Ministry* (ed. P. C. Empie and T. A. Murphy; New York: U.S.A. National Committee of the LWF; Washington, DC: Bishops' Committee for Ecumenical and Interreligious Affairs, 1970)

L–RC 5   *Papal Primacy and the Universal Church* (ed. P. C. Empie and T. A. Murphy; Minneapolis: Augsburg, 1974)

L–RC 6   *Teaching Authority and Infallibility in the Church* (ed. P. C. Empie, T. A. Murphy, and J. A. Burgess; Minneapolis: Augsburg, 1980)

L–RC 7   *Justification by Faith* (ed. H. G. Anderson, T. A. Murphy, and J. A. Burgess; Minneapolis: Augsburg, 1985)

LW   *Luther's Works* (J. Pelikan and H. Lehmann, gen. eds.)

LWF   Lutheran World Federation

TRE   *Theologische Realenzyklopädie*

WARC   World Alliance of Reformed Churches

WCC   World Council of Churches

Preface

What have ecumenical dialogues accomplished, particularly bilateral dialogues between Lutherans and other churches? Have we reached consensus on the gospel? Have we been consistent in what we have said to our various dialogue partners? Have we accommodated ourselves to what our partners in dialogue think, perhaps out of courtesy and friendship?

In order to answer such questions, the standing committee of the Division of Theological Studies of LCUSA at its meeting October 23–24, 1981, authorized a revision of its earlier publication, *Lutherans in Ecumenical Dialogue: An Interpretive Guide.*[1] The study process leading to this publication in 1977 involved the staffs of the Division of Theological Studies of LCUSA and of the Office of Studies of the USA National Committee of the LWF, a consultant, and eight theologians, including representatives of the four dialogues under consideration.

For budgetary reasons the new study did not begin until 1985. Twenty-two theologians plus the staff of the Division of Theological Studies of LCUSA took part in various phases of the process. Teams of two or three, always including at least one person from the dialogue under consideration, prepared analyses of the Lutheran–Roman Catholic dialogue, especially its discussions of teaching authority and infallibility and of justification by faith (1973–1983, held under the auspices of Lutheran World Ministries, formerly the USA National Committee of the LWF), and the six dialogues conducted by LCUSA during 1977–1985. These team reports were discussed and compared in a joint meeting February 1–3, 1985, in St. Louis.

At a second joint meeting in St. Louis, January 10–12, 1986, eight theologians presented essays asking key questions of all seven dialogues. Six of the essays are printed in this volume. James A.

Bergquist, "Mission in Ecumenical Dialogues. Why a Missionary
Framework and Focus Are Indispensable," has already been published,[2] and Gordon Lathrop, "Liturgy and the Bilateral Dialogues,"
was only intended to be a discussion starter and is not included
here.[3] Other key questions could have been asked, such as the
understanding of unity, spirituality,[4] authority, Scripture, and tradition. One essay, in fact, asks what Lutherans find missing in the
dialogues.

The volume concludes with essays by members of the standing
committee of the Division of Theological Studies of LCUSA on the
meaning of ecumenism for their church bodies, the Association of
Evangelical Lutheran Churches, the American Lutheran Church, the
Lutheran Church in America, and the Lutheran Church–Missouri
Synod.

The unanimous "General Findings" of the task force are:

Lutheran churches in the United States which are involved in the
Lutheran Council in the U.S.A. are at different stages or levels, or
at least different stages of articulation, in ecumenical involvement.

a. We recognize the value of all Lutheran bodies, whatever their
stance, being involved in dialogues, both as a way of providing for
the dialogue partner a spectrum of Lutheran views and as a way of
involving each Lutheran group willing to be present. Consideration
might be given, however, to status as observers with full voice rather
than the use of minority reports.

b. In the process of reception of dialogue results it must be recognized that actions are by churches, not by the Lutheran Council (or
by Lutheran World Ministries). Since Lutheran churches are at different stages in ecumenism, we recognize the possibility that one
Lutheran church may have to take the first step toward formal recognition, response, or reception, though it is desirable, where possible,
to have as many Lutheran churches as possible simultaneously taking
common action. The Lutheran–Episcopal agreement on interim sharing of the Eucharist is an example of "church-to-church" overtures
and then of coordinated response. The process of reception is, of
course, also influenced by the wishes of the dialogue partner.

The publication of this volume completes a remarkable "decade
of dialogue," in which Lutherans in the United States through the
Lutheran Council in the U.S.A. and Lutheran World Ministries were

in dialogue with practically the whole ecumenical spectrum: Roman Catholics, Orthodox, Episcopalians, the Reformed, Methodists, Baptists, and, through the Conservative/Evangelical dialogue (which was on a "seminary-to-seminary" rather than "church-to-church" basis), with Mennonites, Nazarenes, the Swedish Covenant tradition, and Wesleyan Methodists. Negotiations for dialogue with the Pentecostal tradition unfortunately did not proceed beyond a preliminary stage. Isolated exceptions to this Lutheran "decade of dialogue," such as dialogue with the Disciples of Christ, were largely a matter of historical convenience and mutual agreement.[5]

Joseph A. Burgess

Introduction:
How to Understand
an Ecumenical Dialogue

Joseph A. Burgess

Ecumenical dialogues come in many shapes and sizes. Each person will have had a different idea or experience. Dialogues between churches at the national level have their own particular dynamics. It is useful to have a description of these dynamics.

Only Official Documents Count

If one has come to know various persons in the Reformed tradition and formed certain opinions about them, does this establish what Reformed teaching is? Lutherans have come to realize that even the majority view discovered through scientific surveys is not an accurate reflection of Lutheran teaching. Official documents have to be evaluated, to be sure, according to what each tradition means by "official," but the decisive point is that dialogues are to be evaluated according to how they have dealt with official documents, not according to how they reflect personal experiences or scientific surveys.

The Human Factor

Each dialogue is unique, like an individual, because each develops out of a unique context and is made up of individuals with their own expertise and agendas. National dialogues do, however, have

11

a kind of official status because the participants have been appointed by the leadership of the churches involved. Lutheran participants know they are to represent the Lutheran tradition even if they have personal reservations.

At the same time dialogue participants do not legislate for their churches, nor should they be understood to imply that they are legislating for their churches. To the contrary, dialogues produce resources that may be useful to the churches; they are doing the churches' "homework," as it were, smashing stereotypes, redis-covering forgotten turns of events, and unraveling past history. On this basis they may make recommendations in order to indicate to the churches what possibilities could now be explored. They speak to the churches, not for the churches. To conclude that Lutherans hold "so-and-so" because a certain Lutheran dialogue has stated "so-and-so" is not necessarily accurate.

In order to be free to explore sensitive issues frankly, dialogue sessions are usually closed to the public. Because the goal is "home-work" and not legislation, participants are normally chosen for their mastery of the material and languages rather than for their repre-sentative function. Dialogue participants work hard together and often become friends, yet this does not mean that they compromise their convictions by finding the lowest common denominator; by and large they hold strongly to their own traditions while remaining friends. Unfortunately dialogue results have at times been skewed by dominating personalities or by devotees; most of the time there is a balance.

Comparing Dialogues

Because dialogue participants have their own personal agendas even while being committed to upholding their own traditions, it is very difficult to compare dialogues. Even within the same series of dialogue there can be inconsistencies based on tensions within the dialogue. This should not surprise, for even within so-called "nor-mative" texts like the Bible these same tensions exist.

Not all dialogues have the same rank even though they may externally look the same, continue for the same length of time, and publish scholarly reports. Certain dialogues have become touchstones, taking on a life of their own. They have been "received" as unusually creative and authoritative. Others have been largely forgotten.

For example, the "Groupe des Dombes," made up of Roman Catholic and Protestant (both Lutheran and Reformed) theologians with some Orthodox involvement, has met in France since 1937. Although not an official church dialogue, its published results are recognized as making a unique contribution to the unity of the church. In 1957 at Arnoldshain, after meeting five times in the preceding ten years, nineteen leading German Lutheran and Reformed theologians agreed on eight theses concerning the Lord's Supper. The New Testament exegetes on the list are world-renowned: Günther Bornkamm, Joachim Jeremias, Ernst Käsemann, K. G. Kuhn, Otto Michel, and Eduard Schweizer. Hardly surprising is the fact that therefore most have held that in dialogues between Lutherans and the Reformed further investigation of New Testament material on the Lord's Supper is unnecessary.[1]

In 1972 the Lutheran–Episcopal dialogue in the United States, in discussing what each tradition had done about apostolicity at the time of the Reformation, stated: "We agree that by each decision the apostolicity of the ministry in question was preserved, and that each of our communions can and should affirm the decision of the other," and then recommended to their respective churches that they consider "II. Agreement that our two communions have maintained the essential apostolicity of the church as set forth in Summary Statement D."[2] This and supporting recommendations began a chain of events leading to the Lutheran–Episcopal Agreement of 1982 between the Episcopal Church in the United States, the American Lutheran Church, the Association of Evangelical Lutheran Churches, and the Lutheran Church in America. Many consider the Lutheran–Roman Catholic dialogue in the United States, which has met since 1965, a kind of bellwether. It has been productive because, among other reasons, it has been given time to develop the methodology and new insights needed to deal with classical issues.

Bilaterals and Multilaterals

Sometimes these two types of dialogue are played off against each other, but each has a different function. Bilateral dialogue has the advantage that comes from two churches focusing on a single theme. The danger is that this will lead to isolation from the larger church, become confrontational, and increase confessionalism. In multilateral dialogue the intellectual complexity increases exponentially and therefore issues may not be pursued thoroughly, but broader perspectives become possible, the larger unity of the church is more of a concern, and it is less confrontational. In actual fact the results of both kinds of dialogue are widely analyzed and compared.

In a similar fashion national and international dialogues are at times played off against each other. Neither, however, ranks above the other, and both are necessary. As with bilaterals and multilaterals, what is decisive is not external status but whether the results of the dialogue do in fact lead to greater insight.

Minority Reports

At first glance minority reports seem out of place and even confusing. It may even seem that someone has refused to be a team player, and this may, of course, have been the case. Minority reports, however, perform an important function in the dialogue process. The Malta Report of the international Lutheran–Roman Catholic dialogue in 1972 has, for example, minority reports from both sides in the dialogue. Minority reports add credibility, demonstrating that the dialogue did not limit itself to the lowest common denominator or force uniformity on everyone.

Ecumenical Strategy

Rumors persist that Roman Catholics have a specific ecumenical strategy, to take a step toward unity with the Orthodox before the end of the century. Such a strategy has a certain logic, yet Catholics assure other Christians that this is not their strategy. Some Lutherans, again according to widespread rumors, hold that Lutheran ecumenical strategy should be to move toward the "catholic" side of the spectrum, toward Rome, Istanbul, and Canterbury. Again, such a strategy has a certain logic, and again, Lutherans assure other Christians that this is not their strategy, but that every ecumenical advance is welcome.

The truth of the matter will be where time and money are spent. The result, to be sure, will also depend on the wishes of the ecumenical partner. Therefore it is crucial to be alert to whatever the ecumenical agenda is and, more significantly, to whatever is neglected. Included in such an examination might be the question of agendas found in bilateral and multilateral dialogues. Why do certain themes recur? Who and what is setting the agenda? Thus both the Lutheran Church in America and the American Lutheran Church criticized *Baptism, Eucharist and Ministry*, for example, for failing to emphasize the centrality of the Word and proclamation and for lacking an adequate understanding of sin and grace and what this means for baptism, Eucharist, and ministry.[3]

Dialogues Need Not Reinvent the Wheel

When certain traditional questions have already been discussed in other dialogues by our dialogue partners, it is not necessary to reinvestigate such questions. Bilateral dialogues are "not intended to produce a comprehensive treatment of all subjects but progress towards practical, bilateral clarification in each case."[4] At times, therefore, a dialogue may simply refer to work accomplished elsewhere, and it is incorrect to demand that each dialogue deal with all questions, even all traditional questions. The standard is not the extensive publication record of the Lutheran–Roman Catholic dialogue, for those publications reflect the very similar investment Lutherans and Roman Catholics have in official theological documents and the need to unravel a long and complex common history.

Specific Terms Are Not Required

Some become upset because dialogue terminology is not what they have been accustomed to. Yet we live in a changing world, and for this reason formulations have to be reformed. Nevertheless, there are those who continue to insist on certain traditional phrases, even in Latin, such as *manducatio oralis* (real eating with one's mouth), when modern phrasing in effect states the same thing. The

Lutheran–Roman Catholic dialogue in the United States in its discussion of the Eucharist has stated the problem *in nuce:*

> It can thus be seen that there is agreement on the "that," the full
> reality of Christ's presence. What has been disputed is a particular
> way of stating the "how," the manner in which he becomes pres-
> ent. . . . Our conversations have persuaded us of both the legitimacy
> and the limits of theological efforts to explore the mystery of Christ's
> presence in the sacrament. We are also persuaded that no single vo-
> cabulary or conceptual framework can be adequate, exclusive or final
> in this theological enterprise.[5]

Ecumenical Context

The rise of the ecumenical movement is commonly described in
terms of key ecumenical events, such as the World Mission Conference in Edinburgh (1910), the founding of the World Council of
Churches in Amsterdam (1948), and the Second Vatican Council
(1962–65). But these events are part of a larger context. Roman
Catholic liturgical renewal began in the late nineteenth century both
in France and Germany. Protestant groups were inspired by this
liturgical renewal, and it gradually became a common project. Protestant use of the historical-critical method, particularly in biblical
studies, made entrenched dogmatic positions less defensible and
lessened the classic polarity between Scripture and tradition. The
encyclical *Divino afflante Spiritu* (1943) made it possible for Roman
Catholic biblical scholars to join publicly in the same kind of biblical
research. Students of Joseph Lortz, whose work *Die Reformation
in Deutschland* (1939–40) challenged Roman Catholic Reformation
scholarship, have opened up alternatives to traditional polemic
against Luther. Just as revival movements of the eighteenth and
nineteenth centuries were of the Spirit but also part of their time,
so the ecumenical movement is of the Spirit but also affected by a
secular world where the church has lost influence and can no longer
afford the luxury of divisions. The ecumenical movement is part of
a world where there are vast secular movements toward unity and
centralization, such as the League of Nations, the United Nations,
and transnational corporations; unity is fostered by new technologies
and global problems, such as instant communication everywhere,

rapid transit to every part of the globe, modern medicine, but also overpopulation and nuclear arms.

The Identity of Identity

Identity means continuity with oneself or itself. How this is to be worked out in practice is not self-evident. Dialogues may strive to eliminate stereotypes and caricatures, but stereotypes and caricatures may also be reintroduced. Where is the control? One attempt to respond to this question is the study report entitled *Lutheran Identity,* produced in 1977 by the Lutheran Institute for Ecumenical Research in Strasbourg.

Generally Lutherans answer this question by referring to the Lutheran Confessions. Yet what does it mean to maintain confessional identity?

> But the assumptions Lutherans have traditionally made about their own theological status can no longer be made. For despite the Lutheran denominations' greater official fervor for their dogmatic tradition, the Book of Concord has little if any greater communal effect among them than do the Thirty-Nine Articles among Episcopalians. . . . The Lutheran denominations live—or do not live—by the same mixture of fundamentalism, helplessness before every wind of doctrine, tag-ends of denominational tradition, and occasional saving theological and proclamatory miracles by which the other American denominations live.[6]

The same point is made less dramatically by the Lutherans in the Lutheran–Roman Catholic dialogue in the United States when they recommend that the Lutheran churches "officially declare that the Lutheran commitment to the Confessions does not involve the assertion that the pope or the papacy in our day is the antichrist." The endnote then spells out what this implies:

> In making such a recommendation we are aware that to the best of our knowledge there is no precedent for Lutherans to affirm officially that, in the light of changing historical circumstances, a statement of the Confessions no longer applies. Our churches, however, have long been involved in such historical interpretation of the Confessions.[7]

One Lutheran approach to this issue is to understand Lutheranism as dynamic, as a developing process. Thus in a sense Lutheranism, in making a theological proposal about justification to the church catholic, depends for its identity on this proposal's "reception," to put it in terms of a current slogan. Does this mean that Lutheranism's identity really lies in the future? But Lutherans have never held that truth lies with the majority or councils or the official church. The Holy Spirit guides the church, to be sure, yet the faith is determined by the gospel, not by reception in the church. The *sensus fidei* is not defined by the *sensus fidelium*.

Most churches, however, do not establish identity through doctrine. As Harding Meyer has trenchantly put it:

> Not only in the Anglican Communion—where it is particularly clear—but also in the constitutional change of the WARC, it is obvious that a certain depreciation of, or at least a slight disrespect for, doctrinal statements of the churches is expressed which we do not share.[8]

How then can Lutherans be in dialogue with nonconfessional churches, where identity is not construed doctrinally? A Consultation on Bilateral Conversations held November 1971 by the LWF in Geneva recommends:

> In particular situations, *communicatio in sacris* and its acknowledgment may properly *precede* the attempt to state doctrinal consensus in the form of agreed statements. A judgment that consent in the gospel and its sacraments exists must precede *communicatio in sacris:* but this judgment may be made concrete in other ways than by explicit propositions about what the gospel is, particularly where the other communion is not accustomed so to proceed. The communions entering fellowship must simultaneously arrange to further in the future their unity in the gospel and Lutherans will expect that these efforts will include doctrinal discussion and formulation.[9]

Anglicans maintain identity through the Book of Common Prayer and church order, the Reformed through church order and new confessions of faith, Methodists through hymnody and their book of discipline. Others maintain identity through particular conversion experiences, life-styles, and symbolic acts. Lutherans may object, for are not books of liturgy and church order changed periodically?

What theology of selection is used for hymns, and who judges conversion experiences and symbolic acts? When, however, Lutherans recall their own need today to apply their Confessions historically, such objections are no longer decisive.

What Is Unity?

Unity is closely related to identity. Unity is "unity," of course, but what is unity like in practice? To be one in fact is part of Christian eschatological hope, as are also the other creedal qualifications of the church—holy, catholic, and apostolic. On this side of the eschaton unity will be limited and imperfect, yet not therefore invisible.

Lutherans have defined the unity of the church in Augsburg Confession 7:

> For it is sufficient for the true unity of the Christian church that the Gospel be preached in conformity with a pure understanding of it and that the sacraments be administered in accordance with the divine Word. (BC 32)

Such a church "actually exists"; it is not "some Platonic republic," (Ap 7:20; BC 171), invisible. The church is rather both hidden and revealed, or is described properly and improperly (Ap 7:17–19, 22, 28; BC 171–73). What is revealed is the pure gospel and the sacraments administered according to that gospel. Further, the exclusory clause, "it is sufficient," makes it very clear that for the "true unity" (CA 7) of the visible church nothing else can be required or necessary, although, as a consequence, great freedom is allowed for whatever seems useful.

What kind of unity the church should have is, to be sure, a matter of continual ecumenical debate. Behind ecclesiological assumptions lie christological, sacramentological, and eschatological presuppositions, all of which are based on views of what is meant by salvation in Jesus Christ. A whole spectrum of models of church unity will be found, often ill-defined, couched in jargon, and admitting of numerous variations: organic unity, conciliarity, unity in reconciled diversity, pulpit and altar fellowship, sister churches, metaphors such as the branch or the type, uniatism, and the like. These models are all earnest attempts to reconcile the call to unity with Christian truth as each holds it. At the one extreme are those contending that such a basic consensus exists that differences are simply questions not yet worked out; at the other are those contending that such basic differences in Christian truth exist that larger unity under most models is unlikely.[10]

The Context of Context

"Context," the modern sense for historical particularity, has been a major tool in ecumenical progress. The appeal to context has opened up the discussion by not allowing the past to be used in a simplistic or dogmatic fashion. At the same time the appeal to context has often been destructive, for it can be relativistic, raising questions about the very possibility of continuity or identity or about whether any basic distinctions can be made. Truth becomes whatever is true for you. It is important to realize that context is part of the modern context, only a tool and not ultimately determinative of truth in general and definitely not of Christian truth. For example, it may be that, when differences are simply attributed to different structures of thought,

> This is clearly an evasion of the issue. Through historical study and imagination it is possible for scholars to learn more than one language and more than one system of conceptuality. It is possible to discern incompatible meanings under the conditions of a plurality of thought structures.[11]

And the arbiter of Christian truth is the Holy Spirit, who "works faith, when and where he pleases, in those who hear the Gospel" (CA 5; BC 31).

Nontheological Factors

Is the ecumenical issue really theological? Is it not really non-theological, based on such factors as entrenched institutions or antiquated philosophical conceptuality? Is anything truly nontheological, however, if it hinders the unity of the church? This really is the issue of non-*doctrinal* factors, of the distinction between doctrine and practice. The question has been around for a long time. No one can deny that nontheological factors are operative.

World trends are often ecumenical trends. As science is guided more and more by statistics, so is every intellectual endeavor, including ecumenical efforts. When the world at large becomes conservative in economics and politics, the ecumenical movement is affected.

More difficult is to discern how such factors can be overcome. Nontheological factors are not necessarily evil in themselves. Further, it is easier to recognize nontheological factors in others than in oneself. And even if recognized, it is hard to escape one's own skin.

What Is Truth?

In an ecumenical context truth is not basically a philosophical question, but the question whether God has spoken and then how to determine what God has said; it is the question of revelation.

For Lutherans the answer is "the gospel," particularly as stated in terms of justification by faith alone in Christ alone.

As can be seen from dialogues around the world, this way of stating the answer is for the most part only a Lutheran emphasis in the dialogues. The major exception is the Agreed Statement by the Second Anglican–Roman Catholic International Commission, *Salvation and the Church* (1987).

Justification is by faith alone in Christ alone; it is a christological proposal. It does not follow, however, as Congar and other Roman Catholics after him claim, that the basic difference between Lutherans and Roman Catholics is therefore Christology rather than justification by faith alone. Birmelé points out that Christology was not in dispute in the sixteenth century and Luther conforms to the Christology of Chalcedon. Congar's real objection is probably to Luther's insistence that justification is by faith alone, God's sole work, which diminishes the role of the church's mediation. It would seem that what is at stake is not Christology but a basic ecclesiological question.[12]

Lutherans are not, to be sure, bound by a particular metaphor of justification. What is decisive is not the conceptuality of justification, but only that, whatever the terminology, salvation be proclaimed by faith alone in Christ alone.[13]

The Future of Dialogue

The era of dialogue is not over. It is just beginning. As the churches move toward acting on dialogue findings, issues will become sharpened and more critical. More dialogue will be needed. The whole life of the church can, in fact, be described as a process of dialogue.

PART ONE

An Analysis
and Evaluation
of Each Dialogue

1

Lutheran–Roman Catholic Dialogue

Carl Braaten
John Johnson
John Reumann

I. Summary of U.S. and International Dialogues, especially since 1977

The U.S. Lutheran–Roman Catholic dialogue is the oldest of all the dialogues to have continued meeting without interruption, from 1965 to date, and is in many ways the most productive. Its first five series of topics were evaluated in the 1977 publication, *Lutherans in Ecumenical Dialogue: An Interpretive Guide* (New York: LCUSA). We note these series briefly as background to the two major topics completed since then, (6) *Teaching Authority and Infallibility in the Church* (1980) and (7) *Justification by Faith* (1983). Included in any analysis of series 7 should be the supporting volume of essays, *"Righteousness" in the New Testament* (1982). The volume *Mary in the New Testament* (1978), produced in the manner of *Peter in the New Testament* (1973) by a Protestant–Catholic task force sponsored by the dialogue, is of only tangential importance for series 6 (which concerned teaching authority and infallibility) as background for the papal dogmas on the Immaculate Conception (1854) and the Assumption (1950); it is possibly of more direct pertinence for the topic begun in series 8 (1984–), "The Saints and Mary."

From the International Lutheran–Roman Catholic dialogue we note as worthy of attention its "Malta Report"[1] entitled "The Gospel and the Church," published in 1972, because of its sections on Justification (§§20–30). We also note in passing the subsequent publications of the Lutheran–Roman Catholic Joint Commission: *The Eucharist* (1980); *Ways to Community* (1981); *The Ministry in the Church* (1982); and *Facing Unity* (1985).

It is to be observed that Lutheran–Roman Catholic relations were in many ways favorably assisted in the period by joint attention to the 450th anniversary of the Augsburg Confession in 1980, the anniversary of Francis of Assisi in 1982, and the 500th anniversary of Luther's birth in 1983.

Publications, vols. 1–7: *The Status of the Nicene Creed as Dogma of the Church* (1965); *One Baptism for the Remission of Sins* (1966); *The Eucharist as Sacrifice* (1967); *Eucharist and Ministry* (1970); *Papal Primacy and the Universal Church* (1974); *Teaching Authority and Infallibility in the Church* (1980); and *Justification by Faith* (1985).[2]

II. Evaluation of Method and Contents

A. Goals. The Lutheran–Roman Catholic dialogue, as was reported in the 1977 guide, continues to operate with considerable freedom, without precisely specified or narrow goals. Informal, annual meetings of bishops and church presidents have helped determine the attention given to important, traditionally divisive issues like infallibility, justification, and Mariology, though the dialogue sets its own agenda and one topic grows out of another.

B. Overall Evaluation. What was said in 1977 continues to be true and can be reiterated about the U.S. Lutheran–Catholic dialogue: its work is impressive to all, scholarly, detailed, challenging, and probably unequaled as a model of theological dialogue. It is to be commended for its regular publication of supporting material, particularly on the exegesis of the Scriptures (as in perhaps no other dialogue) and its historical research. The international dialogue, happily, does not duplicate these efforts but frequently builds on them. All our further evaluative comments, questions, and criticisms must be seen within this basic affirmation of the dialogue's work and a desire for its continued productive efforts in the future.

C. On series 1–5. In reviewing previous work and the comments in the previous LCUSA guide (1977 evaluation), we note:

1. A strength of the dialogue was its practice of indicating places where agreement was not reached or where a topic needed further discussion, as well as cases of consensus, agreement, or convergence.

2. We are happy to note that a concern expressed in 1977, that justification be taken up formally, has now been carried through and that, e.g., the matter of "merit," flagged by the dialogue itself as a topic to be examined in the future,[3] has now been touched on more fully in series 7.

3. However, we also note that on some issues previously discussed, changes have occurred in the treatment of topics over the past generation among both Roman Catholics and Lutherans. As it moves on, a dialogue needs to monitor past agreements and convergences in light of subsequent developments.

To illustrate: in series 1 with regard to what was said about dogma, we may ask whether views have changed in Christology about the "immutability" or irreversibility of the Nicene–Constantinopolitan statements[4] in the light of subsequent hermeneutical discussion.

With regard to the ministry, has consensus in vol. 4 remained as solid among Lutherans (or among Roman Catholics) as it appeared in 1970?

We note also how delicately nuanced footnote material in an earlier volume can later be cited in the text of another document, without offering, however, any further support. For example, series 3[5] presents reactions to Roman Catholic use of the term *transubstantiation* in a series of statements that move from agreement to dissent:

(*a*) Lutherans agree when it is viewed as "affirmation of the presence of Christ's body and blood in the sacrament."

(*b*) Lutherans also teach, although in "different terminology," that "God acts in the eucharist, effecting a change in the elements."

(*c*) They reject it as presumptuous when it is viewed as a "rationalist attempt to explain the mystery of Christ's presence. . . ."

(*d*) They regard it as "theologically untenable" when it is viewed as "a definitive commitment to one and only one conceptual framework. . . ."

On point (*b*), footnote 34 argues that "Lutherans traditionally speak of the change that takes place in the elements as involving a sacramental union with the body and blood of Christ analogous to the hypostatic union of the human and divine natures of Christ," together with the statement "that the bread and wine are essentially untransformed" (citing FC SD 7: 35ff.). Then comes a crucial sentence for later use: ". . . on the basis of Ap 10, 2, which cites with approval the Greek tradition that the bread is truly changed into the body of Christ . . . , there is a certain sense in which one can stand on Lutheran ground and talk about a transformation of the elements. . . ."[6]

This U.S. statement of 1967 has now been quoted in the text of the 1980 international statement *The Eucharist,* ". . . Lutherans also could occasionally speak, as does the Greek tradition, of a 'change.' "[7]

The question remains whether the nuanced U.S. footnote can later be cited as text, even when qualified by "occasionally," and whether Ap 10, 2, does say what is claimed.

D. The sixth series of this dialogue took up the most controversial subject, "Teaching Authority and Infallibility in the Church." With this dialogue and the next one on "Justification by Faith" we are covering two new topics not previously evaluated in the booklet, *Lutherans in Ecumenical Dialogue: An Interpretive Guide.* Our comments will be accordingly more detailed. The dialogue began by building on the useful distinction between the notion of papal primacy and the claim of papal infallibility. Lutherans had conceded in series 6 that under proper conditions the papal office, alongside the episcopal and pastoral offices, could be accepted as a legitimate development in the ordering of the church's ministry. Now Lutherans were being challenged whether they could take an additional step and remove their traditional objections to the dogma of papal infallibility. The Roman Catholic participants softened the interpretation of this dogma to the point that the Lutheran participants responded in an irenic spirit, a far cry from the confessional identification of the papal office as the antichrist.

The dogma of papal infallibility was carefully placed within a comprehensive treatment of the doctrine of authority in the church. With this approach it was possible to show that Lutherans and

Catholics can walk hand in hand a long way before they reach the point of diverging paths. They can agree on the authority of Jesus Christ, the normative role of Scripture, the apostolic tradition, and the creeds and councils of the church, but they cannot agree on the way in which all of these authorities are bound together in the papal exercise of infallible authority. The Catholic theologians gave Lutherans the impression that Vatican II has nuanced the papal claim to absolute authority: "For Catholics, papal infallibility is now commonly discussed in the context of the infallibility of the Church and in relation to confidence in the faithful transmission of the gospel. As a consequence, the infallibility of the Church takes on greater importance than papal infallibility" (§52). Lutherans were assured that "the pope is not an absolute monarch" (§53).

Lutherans, for their part, acknowledged that Roman Catholic teaching as presented in this dialogue no longer teaches infallibility in the sense which Lutherans in the past had to reject as contradictory to the gospel. The Lutherans heard the Catholics to be affirming infallibility in largely the same sense in which Lutherans have confessed the *indefectibility* of the church, namely that "the gates of hell shall not prevail against it" (Matt. 16:18 KJV). Despite the fact that the Catholic side softened the traditional meaning of the dogma of infallibility, it was clear that the Lutherans were not able to grant a consensus, and the Catholics expressed sadness for not being able to reach full agreement with the Lutherans regarding infallibility.

The Lutheran rejection of the infallibility claim need not detract from an emerging interest among Lutherans in regaining an effective magisterium in the church. To be sure, the church does not require an infallible magisterium (cf. §67), nor does the rejection of infallibility imply the rejection of either the papal or episcopal ministries within the church. But effort in regaining an effective magisterium may open up a new appreciation of the role of local pastors, local congregations, and the laity in sharing power and authority in the church (cf. Vatican II's emphasis on the *sensus fidelium*).[8]

Discussion of papal infallibility also raised the question: In what sense do Lutherans regard Scripture as infallible? The Lutheran "Reflections" included the reference from the *Book of Concord* to God's promise in the affirmation "that only the Word of God found in Scripture is 'infallible and unalterable' " (§20; BC 8).

E. The seventh series of the dialogue took up the topic of "Justification by Faith," a theme very close to the heart of Lutheranism.

Two basic achievements in this series are the facts that (1) in its common statement (and there are no separate "reflections" by Lutherans and Catholics, thus heightening what is said together) Lutherans and Catholics have been able to agree together on an affirmation about justification and salvation (§§4, 157) and to make a declaration together (§§161–64) to "Christian believers of all traditions"; and (2) the statement is able to speak together of the gospel, the content of which Lutherans have regularly seen as justification by faith, without using the language of justification and righteousness (see further below).

This dialogue on justification was concluded with rave press reports that Lutherans and Catholics had reached "a fundamental consensus on the gospel" (§164), though they still admitted that even after five years of dialogue they had differences and that "some of the consequences of the different outlooks seem irreconcilable, especially in reference to particular applications of justification by faith as a criterion of all church proclamation and practice" (§121). Questions can be raised about claiming consensus on the gospel if indeed irreconcilable differences on justification do exist, particularly in light of the Lutheran insistence that justification by faith alone is the "article by which the church shall stand or fall." Two currents of thought seem to run through this document; one claims convergence bordering on consensus, the other frankly admits tension and difference. Moreover, at one place the idea of complementarity was suggested, namely, that both traditions, precisely in their opposition, are not contradictory but complementary (§94).

To illustrate, let us have a closer look at some examples. Speaking for Catholics today, paragraph 99 says: "Justification depends on faith, which in turn depends on the word of God, mediated through the Scriptures and the church (cf. Rom. 10:13-17). Receptivity to God's saving word requires that the seed fall on good soil and that the hearer be not deaf." The question from a Lutheran point of view is: Can we use the metaphor of "good soil" to describe the fallen human condition prior to faith?

In §152 it is stated: "What has emerged from the present study is a convergence (though not uniformity) on justification by faith considered in and of itself, and a significant though lesser convergence on the applications of the doctrine as a criterion of authenticity for the church's proclamation and practice." This frank assertion is to be applauded, as is also the statement in paragraph 154: "The Lutheran hermeneutical understanding of justification (§§88–93) in some ways heightens the tension with Catholic positions. It does so by excluding from the gospel proclamation all reference to the freedom and goodness of fallen human beings on the ground that this would undermine the unconditionality of God's promises in Christ. Such interpretation raises even more questions from Lutherans regarding Catholic descriptions of justification as a process of ontological transformation." As an addendum we must point out that the Lutheran hermeneutical position does not exclude "all reference to the freedom and goodness of fallen human beings" (§154).

Paragraph 157 reiterates the agreement stated in no. 4, namely: *"[O]ur entire hope of justification and salvation rests on Christ Jesus and on the gospel whereby the good news of God's merciful action in Christ is made known; we do not place our trust in anything other than God's promise and saving work in Christ."* This is an example of how both sides were able to speak of the Reformation teaching on justification according to which God accepts sinners as righteous for Christ's sake on the basis of faith alone, without using, e.g., forensic terminology, or the term "faith" (cf. "trust" and "hope," however). Compare our comment on 152 above, as a frank assertion of agreement and on how it is not "fully equivalent to the Reformation teaching" (§157).

Lutherans would affirm what is presented as "A Lutheran Hermeneutical Perspective" (§§88–93) because it clarifies Lutheran positions on the relation between faith and good works, on justification and sanctification, and on *simul justus et peccator.*

The Lutheran–Roman Catholic dialogue on justification can teach us a great deal. Its biblical exegetical work was reinforced by John Reumann's companion volume, *"Righteousness" in the New Testament.* The sections in the dialogue on the history of the tradition from medieval to modern times are informative but uneven in quality. A major weakness here was the fact that it barely touched on the Lutheran response to the treatment of justification by the Council of Trent (§§50–57). There was one tiny footnote to Martin Chemnitz's *Examination of the Council of Trent,* but it failed to register the decisive point he made, which in its utter clarity has enjoyed a position of great influence in classical Lutheran theology. This document's survey of the modern contributions to the doctrine of justification (§72) is incomplete. The unparalleled significance of Karl Barth in lifting up this doctrine in twentieth century theology is not mentioned, though his name appears in a long list of Protestants who "have dealt extensively with the doctrine in a wide variety of ways" (§72). The fact that Barth was not a Lutheran is beside the point because Barth on this doctrine has been extraordinarily influential on Lutherans.

We note again that the statement speaks in terms of "consensus" at some points (§164, with reference to §§161–64), but elsewhere the operative form is "convergences" (§§150–60).

However, especially in the popular mind, "consensus" is extended over materials where the dialogue itself at best claims convergence. An underlying assumption in the dialogue is that a certain amount of doctrinal consensus is a prerequisite to altar and pulpit fellowship. A closer examination of the relation between *consensus doctrinae* and *unitas ecclesiae* could be explored in light of the *satis est* principle.

The doctrinal differences between church traditions may be experienced as mutual incentives to expand their horizons and to remain open to fresh points of view. The unity of Christian communities will never develop in history without ambiguities, and such ambiguity will also affect the doctrinal life of the churches. But there must be limits to doctrinal pluralism. Wherever and whenever we in one communion are not able to recognize in another doctrinal tradition an expression of the one hope and the one faith in which Christians believe themselves to be united, then we must separate ourselves from that tradition for the sake of the gospel.

It is clear that our Lutheran participants in these dialogues were fortunately able to acknowledge a common participation in the one body of Christ in spite of some differing forms of belief and teaching. They have contributed to the trend towards unity among Christians, and that is a praiseworthy achievement.

2

Lutheran–Reformed Dialogue

Keith Bridston
Samuel Nafzger

I. Historical Overview

Lutheran and Reformed theologians in the United States have completed three series of formal discussions together. These series of dialogues stand in a certain continuity with each other and may therefore be regarded as a unit. At the same time each series is distinct with respect to such matters as participating churches, operating procedures, and specific mandates.

A. Series 1 (1962–1966)

The first series of conversations, authorized in 1961 by the North American Area of the World Alliance of Reformed Churches Holding the Presbyterian Order (WARC) and the USA National Committee of the Lutheran World Federation, represents the first of the official bilateral dialogues conducted in the USA. The following Reformed Churches participated: Christian Reformed Church, the Orthodox Presbyterian Church, the Presbyterian Church in the United States, the United Presbyterian Church in the U.S.A., and the United Presbyterian Church of Canada. Three Lutheran church bodies were represented: The American Lutheran Church, The Lutheran Church in America, and the Lutheran Church–Missouri Synod.[1]

The historical context of ecumenical optimism within which this first series of discussions took place is significant. For several decades Reformed church bodies had been involved in several successful ecumenical ventures. American Lutherans were also in the midst of a number of family mergers and cooperative endeavors during the early 1960s. These developments affected the direction which this first series of discussions pursued.

The participants in this first series of talks were given the mandate "to explore the theological relations between the Lutheran and Reformed churches to discover to what extent the differences which have divided these communions in the past still constitute obstacles to mutual understanding." It was understood that the individual participants in these talks "would speak for themselves, their conclusions neither necessarily representing nor binding the respective churches which appointed them."[2]

The four sessions in this series of talks discussed papers on these topics: "Gospel, Confession and Scripture"; "Creation and Redemption, Law and Gospel, Justification and Sanctification"; and "Ethics and Ethos." Following consideration of the individual papers, a drafting committee formulated a "summary statement" which presented in thesis form points of agreement and disagreement among the participants. At the fourth and final meeting three supplementary statements were prepared, together with a final "Report to the Sponsoring Confessional Organizations."

Several disagreements were noted: "The place and meaning of law in the new life,"[3] the meaning of "confessional subscription,"[4] "the practice of intercommunion,"[5] "the relation of doctrine to the unity of the church,"[6] "the relationship of the law to the Christian's life" and how "to denominate" God's claim "upon the redeemed . . . whether law or Gospel"[7]; how both to distinguish between while also relating justification and sanctification to one another[8]; and "the importance we attach to the need for the instruction of God's law in the Christian life."[9]

More areas of agreement were listed. They agreed that both Lutheran and Reformed churches "are evangelical in the sense that they are rooted in, live by, proclaim and confess the gospel of the saving act of God in Jesus Christ"; that "the Church is constrained by the gospel to confess its faith"; and that "creedal and confessional subscription is regarded seriously in both Lutheran and Reformed churches."[10] On the doctrine of the Lord's Supper the participants agreed that "during the Reformation both Reformed and Lutheran churches exhibited an evangelical intention when they understood the Lord's Supper in the light of the saving act of God in Christ" and that, "properly interpreted, the differing terms and concepts" which each of these traditions uses "were often complementary rather than contradictory"; that "the presence of Christ in the Sacrament is not effected by faith but acknowledged by faith"; and that "the significance of Christology for the Lord's Supper is that it provides assurance that it is the total Christ, the divine-human person, who is present in the Sacrament, but it does not explain how he is present."[11]

The participants agreed that Jesus Christ is the fulfillment and end of the law and that in the Christian life God continues to lay his claim upon the redeemed"; that "the doctrine of justification by faith is fundamental in both traditions"; that "each tradition has sought to preserve the wholeness of the gospel as including the forgiveness of sins and the renewal of life"; and that "failure properly to interpret and relate justification and sanctification leads to the development of antinomian and legalistic distortions in both traditions."[12] The participants also agreed that there is a common evangelical basis for Christian ethics in the theology of the Reformers" and that "faithful obedience in modern life involves renewed stress on the vital interaction of Christian righteousness and civic righteousness."[13]

In the final "Report to the Sponsoring Confessional Organizations" the participants presented this far-reaching conclusion: "As a result of our studies and discussions we see no insuperable obstacles to pulpit and altar fellowship and, therefore, we recommend to our parent bodies that they encourage their constituent churches to enter into discussions looking forward to intercommunion and the fuller recognition of one another's ministries."[14]

B. Series 2 (1972–1974)

The results of the first series of discussions between Lutheran and Reformed theologians as published in *Marburg Revisited* were sent to the constituent churches. None of the participating bodies, however, took official action to "implement the final recommendation of the first round of discussions."[15]

But in 1971, six years after the first round of discussion had come to an end, it was agreed that a new round of discussions should be undertaken, but this time under the auspices of the newly organized Lutheran Council in the U.S.A. and the North American Area of the World Alliance of Reformed Churches (WARC).

Although the same three Lutheran churches took part in this new series of talks, there were changes in the Reformed delegation. Dropping out of the discussions were the Orthodox Presbyterian Church and the United Presbyterian Church of Canada. New participants in this round of discussions were the Reformed Church in America and the United Church of Christ. Participating in both series were the Presbyterian Church in the United States, the United Presbyterian Church in the U.S.A., and Christian Reformed Church.

The historical context for this second series of dialogues in the early 1970s was significantly different from that of the first series. The spirit of ecumenical optimism which had prevailed in the church had now given way to an atmosphere of caution and reticence.

The dialogue participants,[16] who were appointed to this series of discussions as official representatives of their respective church bodies, were given the following assignment: "In resuming the Lutheran–Reformed conversations, it shall be the objective to assess the consensus and remaining differences in the theology and life of the participating churches as they bear upon the teaching of the Gospel in the current situation."[17]

This second series of dialogue consisted of six meetings held from 1972–1974. Papers were presented on the following topics: Churches in Dialogue Today; *Marburg Revisited;* the Leuenberg Agreement of 1973; and the official position of the participating churches on requirements for admission to the Lord's Table and to pulpits, the role of the Eucharist in the life of the church, and ways to overcome obstacles to fellowship. The results of this series of discussions were presented in a six-page report signed by sixteen of the nineteen participants. The three LCMS representatives, who abstained from signing this report, submitted a minority report which was given to the group but not included in the final revision.[18]

The final report of this series of discussions presents points of agreement and disagreement. The participants concluded that disagreements continue to exist between the Lutheran and Reformed churches relating to the doctrine of the Lord's Supper (1) on "the mode of Christ's presence" in the Sacrament, and (2) on the meaning of "pulpit and altar fellowship." In addition to these specific points of disagreement, it was reported that, having rejected the Leuenberg Agreement of 1973 as the basis for formal agreement between Lutherans and the Reformed in the USA, the participants had also been unsuccessful in finding an alternative to this option. Moreover, they also noted that it had become clear to them "that some of the most intransigent theological differences run across denominational lines." [19]

Despite these differences those participants who signed the final report listed the following areas of consensus: (1) that the Lord's Supper is "a sacrament, a means of grace, in which the true (proper) body and blood of Jesus Christ are present and are eaten and drunk"; (2) that disagreement expressed in their respective Confessions of faith concerning the mode of Christ's presence and in eucharistic practice "ought not to be regarded as obstacles to pulpit and altar fellowship," and that although these differences may "involve error," they "do not amount to heresy and therefore to a denial of Jesus Christ as the one Lord and Savior of Men"; and (3) that "most Reformed churches" and also the ALC and LCA have been practicing open communion and that "these churches practice a measure of pulpit and altar fellowship without formal agreement."

The participants in this series concluded their report by recommending that this series of discussions be terminated, that their churches "approach each other, at every level of life, through a fresh hearing of the gospel declared in Holy Scripture, as well as in terms of their confessional and ecclesiastical traditions," that, if "formal declarations of altar fellowship are desired, this question be dealt with on a church body to church body basis," and that the preaching of the word of God be directed to human needs in the contemporary situation. [20]

The minority report of the LCMS participants, after expressing appreciation for the opportunity to participate in these discussions, says that the dialogue participants had not attained a genuine basis for church fellowship, had not reconciled any existing doctrinal differences, and had not demonstrated valid grounds for accepting the Leuenberg Agreement, but had instead set aside their respective Confessions as viable instruments on the basis of which to declare altar and pulpit fellowship.

C. Series 3 (1981–1983)

None of the participating church bodies responded formally at the church body level to the recommendations of the second series of discussions between Lutheran and Reformed representatives. Nevertheless, early in 1980 the Rev. James E. Andrews, WARC secretary, expressed strong interest to LCUSA's Division of Theological Studies for renewed contacts with Lutherans "because of our common confessional heritage."[21] As a result of this contact, the Division of Theological Studies developed a "Plan for Lutheran–Reformed Dialogue," which was subsequently approved by LCUSA and by the Caribbean and North American Area Council of WARC. In accordance with this plan this third series of discussions, like the second series, was sponsored by LCUSA and WARC.

The Association of Evangelical Lutheran Churches, which was organized in 1976, joined the ALC, LCA, and LCMS in taking part in this series of discussions. Reformed churches participating in this series were The Presbyterian Church (U.S.A.), which came into being during the course of these discussions in 1983 as a result of the merger of the Presbyterian Church in the U.S.A. and the United Presbyterian Church in the U.S.A. (both of these churches had participated in each of the first two series of dialogue), the Reformed Church in America, and The United Church of Christ; both of the latter had taken part in only the second series. Joining these discussions for the first time was the Cumberland Presbyterian Church. The dialogue participants served as official representatives of their respective church bodies.[22]

The "Plan for Lutheran–Reformed Dialogue" describes the purpose of this series as follows: (a) to rediscover the common roots of the heritage of these two confessional families; (b) to examine issues identified as areas of mutual concern, including unresolved issues from previous conversations; and (c) to discover further theological steps we might take together.[23]

In order to accomplish these goals it was decided from the start that six meetings should be held over a period of three years. The final report of this third series of dialogue is entitled *An Invitation to Action*. It includes an introduction, a minority report from the two Missouri Synod representatives, and three joint statements on "Justification," "The Lord's Supper," and "Ministry." Appended to this report are "A Statement of Lutherans to Lutherans Reflecting on This Dialogue" and "From the Reformed Delegation to the Reformed Family of Churches."

The participants in this third series of discussions concluded that some differences in doctrine remain between the two traditions:

> In the past Christians of the Reformed and Lutheran traditions have been deeply divided by controversy over the understanding of the Lord's Supper although both have strongly affirmed the real presence of Christ in the Sacrament. . . . We do not imagine that all differences in eucharistic doctrine between (and within) our two communions have thereby disappeared or become negligible. . . .[24]

In the "Statement of Lutherans to Lutherans" it is stated: "There is no question that there has been and still remains a difference in understanding between Lutheran and Reformed doctrine on the *mode* of Christ's real presence in the Sacrament."[25] Differences in practice, such as the frequency of communion and the use of grape juice instead of wine, persist.[26] The report recognizes that "one of the points at which the Lutheran and Reformed traditions have differed is church order."[27] The Reformed tradition, it is stated, sets "the pastoral office in a broader ministerium," while "the Lutheran tradition has restricted ordination to the ministry of word and sacraments."[28] The dialogue participants note that Lutheran theologians have from time to time criticized the Reformed affirmation of what has been called "the third use of the law."[29] And the final recommendations include the call for "referring any unresolved theological issues, such as the relationship between faith and ethics, and church and world, to a subsequent dialogue."[30]

Nevertheless, despite these differences in doctrine, in theology, in expression, and in practice, the dialogue participants, except for the Missouri Synod representatives, concluded that "there are no substantive matters" concerning "Justification," "The Lord's Supper," and "Ministry" which "should divide us."[31] They hold that differences between Lutherans and the Reformed on "the third use of the law" is not a confessional issue but "rather a difference of theological reflection as much among Lutherans as between Lutherans and Reformed."[32] They conclude: "Our work together in this dialogue persuades us that such a basic consensus now exists among us to justify the conclusion that the condemnations pronounced by the Reformation Confessions are no longer appropriate."[33]

The "Statement of Lutherans to Lutherans" specifically refers to the agreement on the Interim Sharing of the Eucharist between Lutherans and Episcopalians. It is noted that LED II admitted that "to some Lutherans it may seem strange that limited agreement on controverted *loci* should be thought adequate for some degree of ecclesial relationship, when the classical Lutheran position has been that the complete confessional agreement is essential for union." But the "Statement" goes on to report that there has been "some change in some recent Lutheran thinking" on this point.[34] It concludes that the signers of the recommendation were able to discern "no church-dividing issues" between the Lutheran and Reformed traditions: "For our part we see no theological or contextual reasons that now would be impediments to eucharistic and pulpit hospitality and common mission."[35] At the same time the Lutheran participants emphasize that they are not proposing "organic union among churches of the Reformed and Lutheran Confessions." Rather, they state that they are merely setting out "a process of reconciliation."[36]

The representatives from the LCMS did not sign the final report of this dialogue. Instead, as had the LCMS representatives to the second series, they submitted a minority report in which they said that "a number of substantial issues" remained "unresolved." Since the LCMS "establishes altar and pulpit fellowship with other church bodies only after substantial agreement has been reached in all of the doctrines of Scripture," it is stated that they could not concur in the opinion "that Lutheran churches should, at the earliest appropriate time and at the highest level, officially recognize the Eucharists (Lord's Suppers) of those churches which affirm the Reformed Confessions and have them as a living part of their present witness and proclamation."[37]

Although the recommendations made by the first two series of dialogues between Lutheran and Reformed churches received little attention in the participating church bodies, such was not the case with respect to the proposals made by series three. In the summer of 1986 The American Lutheran Church, the Association of Evangelical Lutheran Churches, The Presbyterian Church (U.S.A.), and the Reformed Church in America all took official action to recognize each other as "churches in which the Gospel is proclaimed and the sacraments administered according to the ordinance of Christ," to recognize "as both valid and effective one another's ordained ministries," to recognize "one another's celebration of the Lord's Supper as a means of grace in which Christ, truly present in the sacrament, is given and received," and to allow for "the sharing of pastors" and "occasional joint services" between the two traditions "where appropriate and desirable, and in accord with the disciplines of our several churches."[38] The Lutheran Church in America adopted a somewhat more nuanced proposal which, while providing "for occasional services of the Lord's Supper where appropriate and desirable and in accord with the disciplines of our several churches," calls for additional Lutheran–Reformed dialogues to discuss the Lord's Supper, the nature of Christ, and predestination.[39] (These actions of the ALC, AELC, and LCA are not binding on the new Evangelical Lutheran Church in America. Delegates to a future ELCA convention will be called on to discuss this matter. In 1988 a review committee made up of six from the ELCA and six from the Reformed churches began to prepare recommendations for pulpit and altar fellowship to be ready in 1991.) It should also be noted that the Lutheran Church–Missouri Synod's theological commission prepared a response to *An Invitation to Action* in which support for the minority report of the LCMS participants was expressed.[40]

II. Observations and Questions

A. The Nature of Dialogue: Bilateral or Multilateral?

Observations: From one perspective it is correct to say that the Lutheran–Reformed discussions should be classified as one of the bilateral dialogues. This is an impression that can easily be gained if one looks only at *Marburg Revisited* or if one pays attention merely to the final recommendations of series two and three. But from another perspective it quickly becomes apparent that these discussions more nearly resemble multilateral talks. It should be remembered that the representatives to the first series of discussions made it clear that they were speaking only for themselves and that their conclusions neither represented nor bound their respective church bodies. Once the participants became "official representatives" of their churches, however, the range of differences covered by the labels "Lutheran" and Reformed became more manifest. Two Reformed bodies, the Orthodox Presbyterian Church and the United Presbyterian Church of Canada, immediately dropped out. The Lutheran Church–Missouri Synod, on the other hand, continued to participate in these discussions, but its representatives to each of the last two series of dialogue submitted minority reports in which they strongly dissented from the conclusions and recommendations of the majority. And the rather brief final report of the second series of discussions expressly states that "some of the most intransigent theological differences run across denominational lines."[41]

Questions: How much agreement is necessary on each of the respective sides of the table for bilateral discussions to be productive? To what extent is "intramural" disagreement between dialoguing church bodies an asset or a detriment to progress? How is progress to be measured?

B. The Impact of Dialogue: What Is the Meaning of Reception?

Observations: The first series of discussions concludes: "Our churches are not in full agreement on the practice of intercommunion because they hold different views of the relation of doctrine to the unity of the church."[42] Series two concludes: "We observed that while The American Lutheran Church and The Lutheran Church in America and the Reformed churches adhere to the *doctrine* of the Lord's Supper expressed in their respective confessions of faith, in *practice* they are saying that the confessional differences concerning the *mode* of Christ's presence ought not to be regarded as obstacles to pulpit and altar fellowship. The differences may involve error, but they do not amount to heresy and therefore to a denial of Jesus Christ as the one Lord and Savior of men. These churches practice a measure of pulpit and altar fellowship without formal agreement, and they have done so on the basis of their respective confessions of faith."[43] Series three found no "church-dividing" issues, and the final recommendation calls for "joint celebrations of the Lord's Supper" and filling each other's pulpits, yet it does not recommend declarations of altar and pulpit fellowship and it explicitly rejects any proposal for "organic union."[44] Nevertheless, in the summer of 1986 The American Lutheran Church, The Association of Evangelical Lutheran Churches, The Presbyterian Church (U.S.A.), and the Reformed Church in America decided formally to recognize each other's gospel, ministry, and sacraments. The Lutheran Church in America approved a somewhat more modest proposal.

Questions: What is the relationship between doctrinal agreement and the unity of the church? Is more agreement necessary for organic union than for "eucharistic and pulpit hospitality"? What is the relationship between the latter and pulpit and altar fellowship? What kinds of doctrinal disagreements qualify as "church-dividing?" In view of the fact that it is stated that most Reformed churches and the ALC, LCA, and AELC were already practicing intercommunion, was anything new really being recommended? Are the same standards of "necessary agreement" being applied in all of the bilateral dialogues?

C. The Meaning of Consensus: Disagreements Overcome or Attitude toward Disagreements Revised?

Observations: It is not possible to examine these three series of discussions between Lutherans and the Reformed without asking the basic question: What is really going on here? Lutheran and Reformed theologians came together for theological discussions after many years, even centuries, of antagonism or at best of toleration. They discovered, much to no one's surprise, that there continue to be disagreements between them, disagreements even on such important topics as "the place and meaning of law in the new life," the relationship between justification and sanctification, and "the mode of Christ's presence in the Lord's Supper." To claim then that there are no insuperable obstacles to pulpit and altar fellowship between them raises the strong possibility that what has really taken place in the course of these talks has more to do with the understanding or attitude toward doctrinal diversity than with overcoming differences. This reading of the results of this series of dialogues takes on increased plausibility when the dialogue reports themselves are carefully analyzed. Rarely, for example, is it claimed that "full" agreement has been achieved on the topic under discussion. On the other hand, it is frequently claimed that "fundamental consensus" has been achieved, that "no substantive" disagreements remain, that "strong affinities in doctrine and practice" exist, and that traditional differences are not as serious as they were once thought to be now that we can see that they have been heightened by the use of polemical language which has caricatured, polarized, and masked a deeper, more basic consensus between the traditions.

Question: Are differing views concerning the conclusions and recommendations of these dialogues with the Reformed the result, at least in part, of the failure to make it clear that the recommendations of "eucharistic and pulpit hospitality and common mission" are based more on a reassessment of the significance of traditional doctrinal differences than on their resolution?

D. The Extent of Consensus: Minimal or Maximal?

Observations: After having carefully examined the materials produced by the three series of dialogues with the Reformed, questions arise concerning the absence of in-depth theological treatment of all of the issues which have traditionally separated Lutheran and Reformed churches. The entire report of series 2 consists of only six pages, for example, most of which is taken up in describing procedures and listing recommendations for the future. And the third series seems to have produced surprisingly little new work. This observation is magnified when the materials produced by this dialogue are compared with that which has been produced by the Lutheran–Roman Catholic dialogue, for example.

Questions: Why is this so? Why have the Lutheran–Reformed dialogues resulted in such limited written material? Can this be explained solely by the nature of the dialogues themselves? Such questions, in turn, prompt more basic questions regarding the purposes, functions, presuppositions, methodology, and future strategies of the bilateral enterprise. Who determines the agenda of a bilateral dialogue and on the basis of what criteria? The list of dogmatic or doctrinal issues which have been traditional sources of misunderstanding or causes of conflict or division are one source for setting the agenda. But are these historically determined items sufficient to clarify the root causes of present divisions and separations?

What place should be given to examining philosophical and cultural presuppositions which lie hidden behind dogmatic and doctrinal formulations? The distinctive and peculiar development of Western social, political, and religious institutions needs to be analyzed and evaluated and historically appraised as models of church unity are projected as "goals" for the ecumenical movement and conciliar rapprochement. Does "doctrinal consensus" in fact today, or in history, really provide the essential and indispensable "glue" for ecclesiastical corporate identity? Furthermore, who decides, and how, and on what authority, the degree or gradation of "consensus" required to be certified as authentic "doctrinal agreement"? Attention needs to be given to what actually keeps churches together as compared to what theologically ought to be what keeps them together.

3

Lutheran–Episcopal Dialogue

Robert Goeser
Norman Nagel
William Weiblen

Analysis of the Lutheran–Episcopal dialogue (LED) must begin with a reminder of the history which makes this dialogue different from that with the Reformed and Roman Catholic churches. Dialogue with the latter must attend to doctrinal differences originating in the Reformation, whereas there was no comparable doctrinal conflict between Lutherans and the Church of England; instead, there was considerable proximity in doctrine and liturgy. When seventeenth century Anglicanism came to regard apostolic succession to be defined by episcopal order rather than by doctrine, continental Lutheran and Reformed orders were still recognized and particular regard was expressed for Lutheran orders. The eighteenth century brought closer connections, in part due to the presence of the Lutheran electors of Hanover on the English throne. It was a time of close relations between Lutherans and Anglicans in the American colonies and in India, where Lutheran missionaries served Anglican congregations and ordained indigenous clergy to the Anglican ministry.

Nineteenth century developments moved the two communions further apart. On the one hand, the Anglo-Catholic movement bound apostolicity to episcopal succession and argued for a direct, unimpeachable succession from the apostles to the present episcopacy: catholic ministry and sacraments depend upon episcopal succession.

Accompanying these views of order was a minimizing of Reformation elements in Anglicanism and hostility to Luther and the Reformation. On the other hand, Lutherans in the United States were dominated by a theology of "repristination" which demanded exact doctrinal agreement for any ecclesial recognition. The Anglican and Lutheran expressions alike were part of a resistance to modern thought by establishing an objective authority. Both were searching also for identity in separation from American Protestantism.

Although modern thought and ecumenical discussion had moved both communions from the positions described, the mandate given to the first Lutheran–Episcopal Dialogue (1969–72) was tentative: to define the "possibilities and problems for a more extended dialogue having more specific fellowship" as the goal.[1] However, as the dialogue progressed, remarkable agreement on theological issues and practice led to affirmation of the presence of the gospel and apostolicity in both traditions and recognition that communion with each other would lead to church renewal. The dialogue partners were assisted to these positions by a search for a new language which would not merely repeat earlier propositions.

The summary statements arrived at listed places of agreement, questions to be raised, and actual positions held by the two communions.[2] They thus did not consist of a single agreed text. Four areas were dealt with: (1) The discussion of Scripture recognized common acceptance of the prime authority of Scripture and a historical-critical method of interpretation. (2) and (3) Christian Worship and Baptism and Confirmation were presented as reports on theology and practice in these little disputed areas. (4) The statement on Apostolicity was perhaps the most fruitful in that it moved consideration beyond the issue of historic episcopacy. Apostolicity is manifested in various ways in the church's life, and the substance of succession takes different forms in different times: "Both the Anglican continuity of the episcopal order, and the Lutheran concentration on doctrine, have been means of preserving the apostolicity of the one church."[3] Historically this is a significant statement because it takes the two extreme nineteenth century Lutheran and Anglican positions and maintains that they are not divisive.

Although the dialogue recommended recognition of the apostolicity of both communions and also limited intercommunion,[4] no proposals were brought to the conventions of the four churches.

Concurrent with the American dialogue occurred international conversations (1970–72) authorized by the Lambeth Conference and the Lutheran World Federation. The resulting "Pullach Report" gives a list of agreements which parallel those in LED 1. The agreements are grouped under four headings:[5] (1) *Sources of authority*. The primary authority is Scripture as centered in Christ. The scriptural word is made present in word and sacraments through the Spirit. Tradition is secondary and not an additional source of doctrine. The ecumenical creeds protect apostolic truth, and the sixteenth-century Confessions (including the *Book of Common Prayer*) brought renewal and reforms to the church. Rigorous theological thought is valued; modern theology has brought the two churches closer together than before. (2) *The Church*. The need of visible representation of the church's unity is recognized; both churches are recovering the more dynamic biblical understanding of the church as the people of God. (3) *Word and sacraments*. Reference is made to the nearly verbal agreement on word and sacrament as constitutive of the church expressed in the Augsburg Confession and the Thirty-Nine Articles. The real presence and two sacraments are accepted. (4) *Apostolic ministry*. This is God's gift in Christ to the church, first in the gospel and then in word and sacrament. Apostolic succession is guarded and made contemporary by varied means: Scripture, creeds, liturgy, preaching, confession, sacraments, ordination, pastoral care, and oversight. "The ordained ministry of Word and sacraments is essentially one; all who are called and ordained to this ministry stand together in the apostolic succession of office."[6]

Two elements in this report especially merit comment. First, Christ and gospel are regarded as the heart of Scripture (this formulation is more acceptable than the corresponding formulations in LED 1 and 2). Second, the ministry of word and sacrament is regarded as the essence of apostolic succession. Both expressions are reassuring to Lutheran ears.

The second series of the American dialogue began in January 1976, with misgivings and uncertainty. The failure of the churches to respond to the recommendations of LED 1 instilled doubt about continuing the dialogue. Moreover, although the churches evidently desired further conversation, no clear agenda was suggested.

The main achievement of this dialogue was agreement on five joint statements.[7] The first statements were agreed on rather tentatively; had they been written toward the end of the dialogue they would have received more exact theological articulation. (1) The statement on justification refers to the confessional acceptance in the sixteenth century by both traditions of justification by faith without works. It affirms that in preaching, teaching, liturgy, and sacraments, the two communions maintain God's radical grace in Christ. (2) The statement on the gospel is primarily a review of the history of salvation; coupled, however, with the statement on justification, the gospel intention is evident. (3) The statement on Scripture affirms its normative character for both communions. It expresses the centrality of Christ in Scripture, although obscurely because inspiration rather than revelation is emphasized. No reference is made to modern biblical scholarship.

The most fully developed statements are those on eucharistic presence (4) and apostolicity (5). They include considerable documentation in response to the criticism of LED 1 regarding the lack of documentary support. The statement on eucharistic presence reflects recent liturgical and biblical scholarship; emphasis shifts from the substance of the elements to the event of new creation realized by word and Spirit in the life of the people of God. This reality both points back to the saving event in Christ and forward to the eschatological union in Christ. The statement on apostolicity reiterates the view of LED 1 and the international conversations, that apostolicity is present in varied ways. Attention was drawn to the considerable agreement in understanding ordained ministry: the divine institution of the ministry of word and sacrament, the practice of ordination, succession in the office of ordained ministry, and the need for oversight.

The dialogue recognized that the joint statements are not full Confessions of faith; they do not say all that either church would wish to say. They reassure each other, however, of fundamental doctrinal agreement at significant places; what is doctrinally crucial for one church is being affirmed by the other.[8]

On the basis of the joint statements the dialogue made the following recommendations to their churches: (1) that there be mutual recognition of each other as "true Churches where the Gospel is truly preached and the sacraments duly celebrated"; (2) that a policy of interim eucharistic hospitality be effected; (3) that local congregations be involved in appropriate shared services of worship; and (4) that local congregations cooperate in prayer and in programs of education, mission, evangelism, and social action. The representatives of the Lutheran Church–Missouri Synod demurred from these recommendations.[9]

The churches did act in response to these recommendations. In September 1982 the conventions of the Episcopal Church, the LCA, the ALC, and the AELC voted (1) to recognize each other as "Churches in which the Gospel is preached and taught," (2) to "encourage the development of common Christian life" through mutual prayer, study of Scripture, and programs of religious education, theological discussion, mission, evangelism, and social action, and (3) to affirm the studies of LED 1 and 2 and the Anglican–Lutheran International Conversations as indicating teachings consonant with the gospel in each church which justify a declaration of "interim sharing of the Eucharist." Guidelines were then spelled out for this sharing.[10]

This action is notable in three respects. First, this is the first bilateral dialogue to lead officially to "substantive interchurch agreement and activity." Second, the action of the churches came not from more thorough theological discussion and documentation by LED 2 but from a changed historical situation. Third, the action represented a shift from nineteenth century views and positions.

It is instructive again to observe the report of the Anglican–Lutheran European Commission (1980–82). Its first statement is on justification and is ordered much like that of LED 2 (and quotes from the latter). It consists of a longer statement on the nature of alienation in contemporary life and of the relevance of justification to provide reconciliation, meaning, and freedom. The doctrine is recognized as fundamental to the Reformation heritage of both communions. The statement on baptism recognizes divine initiative and personal appropriation. The discussion of the Eucharist observes that there has never been a substantial difference between the two traditions at this point. Both recognize in the whole celebration the true presence of Christ as God and man, crucified, risen, and ascended, under the elements of bread and wine. Allowing for differences in the doctrinal role of the liturgy, the statement concludes that the common tradition of spirituality, liturgy, and sacramental life provides a basis for mutual recognition of church, sacrament, and ministry. The statement on ministry and episcopacy maintains that there has been rediscovery of much common ground here and that there had never been deep ecclesiological differences. Apostolicity again is seen as expressed in varying ways and belonging to the whole church.[11]

What brings these churches together is not so much particular doctrinal agreement as common configuration: high regard for sacramental life and liturgical worship, affirmation of church as community, historical sense regarding the development of the church, historical study of Scripture, and a generally conservative political and social stance which has sometimes impeded the development of profound social conscience and sense of mission. Both have a strong theological tradition, but with significant differences. Lutherans are given to confessional allegiance and doctrinal definition. (In this they are more akin to the Reformed and Roman Catholics.) Theological content centers on sin and grace. Anglicans are more influenced by the Greek fathers and Platonism; they are especially concerned with the incarnation and natural theology. The profound Lutheran theology of grace and incarnation is oriented differently. Perhaps what most distinguishes them (despite common Reformation and catholic elements) is the way the word is the source of theological and ecclesiastical coherence for Lutherans, and liturgy and order for Anglicans.

What remains is for the churches to move toward full communion. Certain moves are under way. The Anglican Consultative Council and the Lutheran World Federation have appointed the Anglican-Lutheran International Continuation Committee, a continuation of the Anglican–Lutheran Joint Working Group that had met under the same auspices at Cold Ash, England, late in 1983. The task of the Continuation Committee is to "coordinate information about developments in Anglican–Lutheran relations" throughout the world and, having assessed the total situation, "to foster and stimulate new initiatives."[12] The Continuation Committee has drawn attention to an "ever-increasing closeness of relationship" at the regional level in Tanzania, Canada, Europe, Australia, and India as well as in the United States of America.[13] This same committee held a consultation on *episcopé* at Niagara Falls in September 1987. The Niagara Report itself is not a report of the consultation but of the Continuation Committee as it met after the consultation. Notable is the emphasis on mission as the guide to how *episcopé* is to function.[14] In an attempt to find ways around traditional difficulties with the historic episcopate, concrete steps are proposed: Lutherans are asked to use the title "bishop," to have bishops without limit to their term of office, to have at least three bishops lay on hands when a bishop is installed, and to have only bishops preside at ordinations; Anglicans are asked to "recognize the full authenticity of the existing ministries of Lutheran Churches," to review episcopal ministry periodically, and to invite Lutheran bishops to participate in laying on hands at the consecration of Anglican bishops.[15] Further reflection will come from the Lutheran and Episcopal churches as they ask themselves to what extent they are able to receive such proposals.

The first phase of the third series of the Lutheran–Episcopal Dialogue in the United States of America met from 1983 to 1988. Its mandate, given by the Lutheran and Episcopal churches in the Agreement of 1982, is to take up the implications of the gospel, the historic episcopate, and the threefold ordering of ministry in the total context of apostolicity. With the publication of *Implications of the Gospel*[16] the first phase has been completed. It is a long statement, using contemporary, dynamic theological language, aimed at stimulating study and renewal in the churches.

The first section describes Jesus' proclamation of the reign of God, based on a hope grounded in the resurrection and defined by the cross. The second section identifies both Christology and the Trinity as doctrines of the gospel. The third section takes up the church and its functions as necessary implications of the gospel. The final two sections deal with the gospel and the world and the mission of the gospel in the world. The five sections provide an "integrative focus for various facets of the church's life," and specific recommendations are made concerning worship, ecumenism, evangelism, and ethics in order "to make our churches more faithful in their life and witness."[17] The representatives of the Lutheran Church–Missouri Synod made a separate report.[18] The second phase of the dialogue, on the historic episcopate and the threefold ordering of ministry, has now begun.

4

Lutheran–Methodist Dialogue

Timothy F. Lull
Alice L. Schimpf

I. Themes of the Lutheran–Methodist Dialogues

In comparison to some of the dialogues that have continued for a longer time, the Lutheran–Methodist conversations have produced a modest literature. Perhaps this is not surprising. Lutherans and Methodists are neither nearest ecumenical neighbors, by most accounts, nor so distant in their approaches that dialogue between them seems remarkable.

This will be readily apparent to anyone who thinks about these two churches. The Methodist strength has been in Britain, in the United States, in other English-speaking nations, and in former mission churches in various parts of the third world. Lutherans, on the other hand, can be found in the old Lutheran churches of Germany and the Nordic countries, in the United States and Canada, and in a number of third world countries which were mission territories or which received settlers from traditional Lutheran lands.

Therefore it is not surprising that the first series of official dialogue took place within the United States. In six meetings lasting from 1977 until 1979 the dialogue group made a careful study of baptism. The format for the published statement, kept brief to allow wide circulation, precluded acknowledgment of such commonalities as

Scripture as the source and norm of faith, the Trinity, acceptance of justification, and use of the sacraments as "means of grace."

This series issued a very modest set of conclusions emphasizing affirmations rather than areas of disagreement. Its particular emphasis on practical implications was part of a strategy of speaking directly to the churches, with special interest in practical implications.[1]

Spurred by the good results in the United States, another dialogue took place at the international level, sponsored by the World Methodist Council and The Lutheran World Federation. In meetings from 1977 until 1984 a greater range of topics was discussed than those covered in the U.S. first series report. The conclusions of this international series can be found in *The Church: Community of Grace*.[2]

A second series of U.S. talks (1985–87) resulted in a report *Episcopacy: A Lutheran/United Methodist Common Statement to the Church*. This report takes up quite a different set of issues than the first two documents. This is an especially useful development because these topics have also been discussed in a number of the other bilateral dialogues.[3]

II. Baptism (The U.S. Dialogue, First Series)

Lutherans and Methodists seem to have started their U.S. dialogue with a relatively easy ecumenical topic. Baptism had been a good beginning or early topic in other dialogues (Lutherans and Roman Catholics had done well with this topic in their second series of talks in 1966), and there were no apparent deep differences in the practice of baptism. Nevertheless, one representative of the Lutheran Church–Missouri Synod disagreed enough with the direction to dissent from their conclusions throughout the process.

The document speaks of certain presuppositions or foundations for agreement on baptism and lists first acknowledgment of "Scripture as the source and norm of Christian faith and life" and "that Christology and that Trinitarian faith which are set forth in the ecumenical Apostles' and Nicene Creeds" (#2). This must have been helpful to those Lutherans who could have doubts about whether

Methodists, who appear quite pluralistic in theology, hold today these traditional commitments of the Methodist church.

The Reformation is also seen as a common heritage helpful for a statement on baptism, but this has to be phrased in a somewhat cautious way to take into account the critique of Reformation theology which has been important in Methodism since its beginnings. Therefore "justification by grace through faith" is affirmed as "the biblical Reformation doctrine" which both churches share. This affirmation of justification is balanced by a recognition of "the common emphasis on sanctification as a divinely promised consequence of justification." This may be strong language for some Lutherans, but it probably is reassuring to many Methodists that justification is not to be understood in such a way as to leave an opening to "cheap grace."

Moreover, on the crucial question of sacramental efficacy the statement says: "We affirm that God acts to use the sacraments as means of grace" (#2). This statement is important to remember in tension with the strong emphasis on baptismal responsibility found in much of the later part of this Statement.

In fact, throughout the Statement careful attention has been given to include affirmations of Lutheran concerns for grace (received in faith) and Methodist concerns for human faithfulness (enabled by grace). Paragraph 10 seems to be at the heart of the theological compromise achieved here:

> We affirm that in claiming us in Baptism, God enables the Christian to rely upon this gift, promise, and assurance throughout all of life. Such faithful reliance is necessary and sufficient for the reception of the benefits of Baptism.

This formulation deserves careful study, especially from the Lutheran perspective. Lutherans have been reluctant to claim for baptism a kind of magical efficacy that made the benefits of baptism follow automatically. But Lutherans also sense the danger of making faith the actualizing power of baptism, eclipsing the divine initiative at the heart of the sacrament. In this dialogue Lutherans and Methodists worked together to maintain this proper tension.

There are other important features of the common statement. The diverse benefits of baptism are recognized, with a strong statement about forgiveness of sins but with careful attention to ways of expressing baptism's effect on the baptized person (#9). Baptism is affirmed as the "sacrament of entrance into the holy catholic Church," and the dialogue partners are urged to see in the actual practice of their existing recognition of each other's baptisms a sign that there must already exist a unity which permits such recognition, a unity which deserves articulation and ecumenical celebration (#6).

As would be expected, the dialogue affirms infant baptism, which has been the practice of both communities. The reason given for this appears to be that the church should include all persons, "even infants" (#8). This does not express fully the reasons for which Lutherans have wanted to affirm infant baptism (including the terrible power of original sin, as expressed in Article 2 of the Augsburg Confession).

Nor does the document seem to have gone very far in mounting the kind of vigorous defense of the practice of infant baptism which may be important in a society (like the U.S.) where the criticism of this approach is so strong from Baptist and other churches. Both Lutherans and Methodists have to meet that challenge if they (and other churches retaining catholic practice at this point) are to continue to be persuasive in their reasons for baptizing infants.

The document concludes with a list of implications and recommendations for baptismal theology and practice which it is hoped can be shared with enthusiasm by Lutherans and Methodists alike. Private baptism is rejected; Christian nurture is affirmed. The problem of baptism where one parent is Methodist and the other Lutheran is discussed with sensitivity to the ecumenical complications from the child's point of view. Baptism cannot be repeated, but the mode of applying the water is an open question.

Two of the other recommendations are a bit more complex. One has to do with the nature of confirmation. The Statement affirms that baptism is complete in itself (when the baptized person is one who has been instructed and has made a profession of faith) and that no separate rite is needed (#17). The statement affirms the diversity of understandings between (and within) these churches regarding confirmation and says that these can be respected (#18).

The other complex issue has to do with the baptism of children of nonchurch members. These churches want to distance themselves from what has often been called "indiscriminate infant baptism," and the test here proposed is that the baptism of an infant should only take place in those circumstances where "at least one adult parent, surrogate parent, or other responsible adult" makes a commitment to nurture this child in the faith. Sponsors are considered an inadequate substitute for parental commitment (#14).

It would seem that this could be interpreted pastorally in both generous and very strict ways and might in fact cover over divergent views of the desirability of infant baptism or the sense of what real Christian commitment represented. There is no hint in the statement that an arbitrary use of "qualifications" by pastors might undercut the very language of grace so prominent in the opening paragraphs.

III. The Church: Community of Grace (International Dialogue)

The international study is much broader in scope and much more ambitious in its intentions than the First Series of U.S. dialogue. It built on the success of the first series of U.S. conversations, with some of the same persons involved.

The document contains five sections which summarize the several years of theological talks and concludes with suggestions for the future and recommendations to the churches. Here the scope is much richer than in the U.S. dialogue, but a disadvantage comes in the number of major issues which must be covered in a relatively short space.

The first section deals with "The Authority of the Scriptures." Jesus Christ is "the Word of God incarnate" and Scripture is "a faithful witness to this central revelation." The Bible is the "most authentic, faithful, and trustworthy bearer of the Word of God." It is the criterion of judgment for each of our traditions (#15).

Scripture is diverse and must be studied and interpreted critically, always with reference to "Jesus Christ as the Lord and Savior, its authentic center and content" (17). Distinctions must be made within Scripture, and Christ is the key to these. As has been true in most dialogues, there is no real exploration of the traditional Lutheran theme of law and gospel as a tool for learning what points to Christ. Here, without a distinction of levels, Scripture is the source of "primary authoritative standards" not only for faith, but also for "life, witness and work" (#16).

Tradition, reason, and experience each have their role to play in the interpretation of Scripture (#18–#21). The statement artfully shows how each of these has been used in both Lutheran and Methodist churches in diverse ways. Perhaps this elaboration of the working out of Scripture's authority works better for Methodism (with its Anglican roots) than for Lutheranism (whose attitude toward tradition, reason, and experience has been very dialectical).

The section ends with a reminder that while Lutheranism has been shaped by Luther and Methodism by Wesley, it is dangerous to see either tradition in too simple a relation to the "founder." Various social and cultural forces have also shaped each church, and various styles of piety have been known in each. Some Methodists may have more in common with some Lutherans than with other Methodists, as well as the reverse (#22).

The second section deals with the crucial question of "Salvation by Grace through Faith." The statement moves forward by a series of listings of ways that Lutherans and Methodists have seen the various aspects of this salvation, with occasional common affirmations.

The opening agreement is the key to what follows:

We agree that, in accordance with the Scriptures, justification is the work of God in Christ and comes through faith alone. Within the context of justification, faith comprises both assent and trust. Persons as sinners are justified by God's gracious love in Christ, and not on the basis of human efforts or worthiness. Christ's righteousness is imputed and imparted to them by an act of God as they are enabled by the Holy Spirit to trust in God. Justification is dependent upon Christ's atoning death. In Christ God reconciled the world and conquered the evil forces that dominate human life and the created order. (#23)

This statement skillfully weaves together important emphases from each tradition. How then is the characteristic difference in emphasis between the traditions explained?

This is clearest in the paragraphs dealing with sanctification. While a major common core of belief is asserted even here (#25), there is an admission that Lutherans have tended to stress the reality of remaining a sinner while Methodists "dare set no limit to what the grace of God can do for people in this present life." This more detailed spelling out of diverse theologies of the Christian life is a helpful expansion of the rather bold claim by the U.S. dialogue of "the common emphasis on sanctification as a divinely promised consequence of justification" (#2).

The third section discusses "The Church." While there are complex issues lurking here involving ministry, order, discipline, and social context (some of these taken up in the subsequent second U.S. series), this section assumes a large measure of agreement. Both churches celebrate ordered ministry and the function of episcopacy in the church without making these essential marks of the church (##38–39). Lutherans express regret for past excesses of state churches in inhibiting religious freedom for Methodists (and others) (#34).

The fourth section, "Means of Grace," comes to the complex sacramental issues of the understandings of baptism and Eucharist within each tradition. The baptismal section builds on the work of the U.S. dialogue (acknowledged at #85) and at two crucial points improves upon it.

One of these is the explicit statement that faith, so important in relationship to baptism, is itself a gift of the Holy Spirit. "The Holy Spirit enables human beings to rely faithfully upon God's promise of grace expressed in the sacrament" (#46). This protects against the danger of faith becoming the ultimate good work rather than trust in God's graciousness.

The other key point is the admission of a difference between the traditions in the human ability to come to baptism and a clear spelling out of the Methodist sense of "an anticipatory effect enabling positive response of human beings." Lutherans have been reluctant to speak of such anticipation, lest it undercut grace by an undue elevation of the human role in baptism (#50).

In treating the Eucharist, the document acknowledges that both traditions share a catholic heritage, a strong sense of Reformation theology, and a current reshaping of eucharistic thought and practice. Both are said to see the sacrament not only as outward but also as "an effective sign of the presence of the risen Lord Jesus Christ. His presence is real here and now" (#54).

But for all that commonality and for all of Wesley's high view of the sacrament, there are differences between the traditions at this point. These are expressed largely in terms of a contrast between a Lutheran emphasis on "the real yet mysterious union between Christ's body and blood and the elements" and a Methodist sense that it is those who believe who receive the body and blood of Christ (#54). While bread and wine are mentioned as the elements, no recognition is made of the widespread use of grape juice in U.S. Methodism.

The final, longest section of the document deals with "The Mission of the Church." Evangelization and issues in Christian ethics are the major concerns in this part. The responsibility of the church to preach the gospel and to witness to society are each held forth eloquently. And yet this section is perhaps the least successful of the whole document.

For by comparing the contemporary ideals of each church, the impression is given of a commonality which is hard to sustain in looking at the history of each group or even much contemporary parish practice in the U.S. Is enough recognition given to the struggle of Lutherans in recent decades toward Christian social responsibility? Is there any hint that U.S. Methodism sometimes showed a tendency to move away from the "joy and freedom of the Christian life" (#74) toward a rigid and predictable code of personal morality?

The document concludes with suggestions and recommendations. A number of concrete suggestions for common study and sharing of resources are complemented by a suggestion that future dialogues could pursue unresolved theological issues such as two kingdoms, anthropology, and the form of unity.

But the recommendations are striking. In contrast to the modest recommendations of the U.S. dialogue, this study suggests "steps to declare and establish full fellowship of word and sacrament" (#91). This could begin with pulpit exchanges and "mutual hospitality at the table of the Lord." This may be something less than the "interim sharing of the Eucharist" of U.S. Lutherans and Episcopalians and surely is something more than a commitment to common service and future common study.

IV. Episcopacy: A Lutheran/United Methodist Common Statement

A second series of U.S. dialogues was held in the years 1985–87. The topic selected was episcopacy, for reasons not altogether clear from the document. In any case the choice was a good one at a time when both traditions were being asked to think about such questions as the threefold office and apostolic succession by the "Ministry" proposals of *Baptism, Eucharist and Ministry.*

In this dialogue Lutherans and Methodists seem to have found themselves on common ground, perhaps even forging a common front. The report takes what might be called a "low" or evangelical view of episcopacy, as opposed both to the traditional high views of Roman Catholics and Anglicans and the general reliance on non-episcopal structure to meet this need in much of the Reformed tradition.

The theological rationale for this approach is found in a common question that both traditions want to ask about the general nature and structure of any ministry: "do they further the fundamental mission of the Spirit within the church?" (#10).

Traditional oversight through bishops is affirmed as "theologically and practically desirable" but not "the exclusive prerogative of the bishop" (#17). That authority which bishops possess must be carried out "in cooperation with other persons within the church" (#17) and with clear acknowledgment that it is subordinate to "the authority of the Bible" (#19). For the sake of mission throughout the world "we must be open to different forms of oversight" (#13).

While the document shows evidence of readiness to debate new proposals about episcopacy for the sake of the unity and mission of the church, Lutherans and Methodists here seem to be formulating a common approach. Three conditions are set down: (*a*) that mission must be served by any change, (*b*) that it cannot be implied that anything essential has been lacking in the past ministries of these churches, and (*c*) that such reordering cannot be seen as "of the essence of the church."

These conditions seem to set very clear limits for how far these churches could stretch their understanding of oversight and of continuity and unity served by episcopal succession. Lutherans will need to have extensive discussions of these conclusions to be sure that they are consistent with what they have said to other communions and in current theological work.

But the special service of this dialogue may be to show how difficult it is to pack everything into the doctrine of justification as the sole criterion for the completeness of reform within a reuniting church. In a way that still needs exploring, Lutherans (and Methodists) should consider whether some second principle—structural freedom or legitimate churchly diversity—is needed to stand alongside the proper understanding of justification in forming the church's present and future life.

V. Theological Reflections on Achievements and Limitations

A major advantage is that this dialogue has brought together churches who have neither a history of warfare nor of close commonality, but who are middle-range ecumenical neighbors. This is even more interesting because of some of the complementary weak spots and points of tension between these churches. The dialogues give evidence that the participants not only enjoyed the study but learned in both directions. Here Part II of the most recent statement, "Practice of *Episcopé* in the Two Traditions" is an especially helpful piece of descriptive ecumenical work.

One considerable achievement is in the comparison of unlikes. The international dialogue is eloquent about the difference between these churches (#8). And yet ways have been found to consider not only foundational theological documents (so crucial for Lutheran self-understanding) but also present churchly realities and patterns of piety and ethos.

Lutherans and Methodists have been learning that they complement each other in some very significant ways. For example, in relation to evangelization the international dialogue makes the following suggestion:

> Methodism may profit from Lutheran concern for the clarity of the gospel; Lutherans may be inspired by Methodism to implement their evangelistic impetus. (#57)

Each of the dialogues makes its own contribution to the wide, emerging ecumenical consensus. The first U.S. document stresses practical ecumenical issues at the parish level. The international dialogue struggles to articulate a common theological core for two traditions remote enough from each other to have no easy access to such statements. If there are limits to the success of this enterprise, there is also an impressive level of accomplishment. The second U.S. document prepares the way for future discussions of ministry and authority on an even broader level.

A balanced account must also mention limits and even weaknesses of these dialogues. Each worldwide communion is very diverse within its own membership. This is apparent for Methodists where one often sees a real theological difference between British and American Methodism, for example. But it is equally true on the Lutheran side.

In the case of the first U.S. dialogue representatives from the Lutheran Church–Missouri Synod abstained or voted "No" on the common statement. In the case of the international dialogue the Missouri Synod did not participate (not being a member of the Lutheran World Federation) and here also one of the Lutherans dissented, The Rev. Lars Ostnor of Norway. Perhaps surprisingly, the Lutheran Church–Missouri Synod representatives did vote in favor of the second U.S. agreement.

But failure to reach consensus is not the only danger here. There is a need to check the reality of agreements against the actual reality of the faith and commitments of the churches today. Perhaps there is a special danger at this stage of the ecumenical movement of saying "Yes" in order to be helpful, in order not to put obstacles, because of a sense of embarrassment about the concreteness of one's own tradition. (This says nothing to another danger, that those selected for bilateral dialogues may in fact be among those within each tradition who have special affinity for the other tradition. That can lead to exciting new formulations, but it needs to be checked by reality.)

The diversity of Christian voices is in one respect the result of sin and needs the healing power of the Holy Spirit leading toward unity. But this particularity is also an enrichment of the church catholic. Having all Christians speak alike on complex issues like

sacraments or justification or Christian social responsibility or episcopacy may be as much impoverishment as healing.

In the end the success of the dialogues depends on the consent
of the faithful in the churches and the consistency of these results
with that which has been achieved in other dialogues. The progress
for Lutherans and Methodists is real and welcome. But whether it
is a major or minor accomplishment will in the end depend both on
implementation and on broader developments in the ecumenical
situation.

5

Lutheran–Baptist Dialogue

Delmar Gusdal
Paul Jersild

I. Introduction

This dialogue was initiated in September 1977 when "A Plan for Lutheran–Baptist Conversations" was drawn up by staff members of LCUSA and the North American Baptist Fellowship,[1] the latter being an association of seven Baptist bodies in the U.S. and one each in Canada and Mexico.

Formal papers on selected theological topics were presented at each meeting by each side. By the conclusion of the sixth and final meeting the participants had prepared three common statements entitled "Divine Initiative and Human Response," "Baptism and the Theology of the Child," and "Church and Ministry." These statements, together with recommendations to the sponsoring bodies and a number of individual papers, were published in the *American Baptist Quarterly*.[2]

Relatively modest goals were adopted. The word "conversations" was chosen to describe these meetings, but it yielded at an early stage to the more traditional term "dialogue." This term was symbolic of a growing awareness in both groups that a significant "day one" might be occurring, with possible historic implications. It is relevant that during 1980–1981 a series of four meetings ("Baptisten und Lutheraner im Gesprach") was held in Germany between representatives of the *Vereinigte Evangelisch-Lutherische Kirche Deutschlands* and the *Bund Evangelisch-Freikirchlicher Gemeinden in Deutschland,* a group of Baptist and Brethren congregations.[3] An international dialogue on the part of the Baptist World Alliance and the Lutheran World Federation will make its final report in 1990.

II. Content of the Dialogues

At the first meeting a general overview of agreements and disagreements was shared. Two themes came to the fore and continued to be prominent throughout the dialogue: (1) Primary was the centering of Lutheran theology on justification and of Baptist theology on regeneration. These commitments in turn set the course for the diversity of other theological understandings and the differences of ecclesiastical life-style that characterize each communion. "Justification" has in a very special way been determinative for Lutheran history as has "regeneration" for Baptist history. Each has had a respective effect upon doctrine, policy, worship, and life in the secular world. (2) Another important theme was the impact of history in the shaping of each tradition. The first of the three common statements, "Divine Initiative and Human Response," deals with "Backgrounds to Differences."[4] The most formative influence for Baptist developments was seventeenth century English congregationalism in the context of an Anglican state church. In this setting of early Puritan developments regeneration and commitment came to the fore. Lutheranism's reaction to sixteenth century legalism shaped its quest for a gracious God and emphasis on the justification of sinners. These two concerns were seen as conditioning the development of each church. Lutheran concern for giving glory to God and comfort to repentant sinners led to an emphasis on the action of God in justification. Baptist concern for repentance and conversion led to an emphasis on faith as a human response to divine initiative.

Subsequent discussion focused on the following topics: faith and experience, sacraments/ordinances, faith in the theology of the New Testament and in each of the traditions, the nature of the church and ministry, baptism and its relation to conversion, baptism and the theology of the child, and infant baptism in relation to sin, Bible, church, faith, tradition, and sacrament/ordinance.

A. *Baptism*

These historically conditioned and divergent emphases became most obvious with regard to baptism. "Baptists see believers' baptism as most consonant with a concept of a regenerate church. . . . Lutheran theology continues to carry through the theme that the action is primarily divine. In adults the Spirit works faith through the hearing of the word and through baptism; for infants the activity of the Spirit begins with Baptism and leads to their confession of Jesus as Lord."[5]

Lutherans continue to stress the priority of the external means as "God has determined to give the inward (through the Holy Spirit, faith and other gifts) to no one except through the outward."[6] These external means are not in opposition to faith nor do they detract from it, for faith is essential to receive and enjoy the gift. The sacraments, along with the preached word, mediate the promise and arouse and strengthen faith. But the validity and dignity of God's Word and of the external signs are independent of our faith.

The recurrent interest in baptism led to a discussion of the theology of the child. Baptists and Lutherans both recognize a child's solidarity with Adam in death, but the Baptist representatives indicated that children are culpable before God only when, of their own will, they are able to depart from God. Children of believing parents are born within the bosom of the church and are to be taught the faith until they make their own confession in baptism.

The Lutheran tradition was represented as teaching that the reality of sin is expressed from the beginning of a person's life. God's promise in Jesus' death and resurrection is effectively applied to children in baptism where they are incorporated into Christ.

In summary: it became apparent that Lutherans insist that baptism effects what it signifies. Baptists in turn gratefully recognize the operation of grace in faith, but they see that as exhibited precisely in the baptism of the believer who has responded to grace. The point of difference was sharply put in the common statement: "Baptists regard the believing response of infants to be an unwarranted hypothesis and Lutherans regard the idea that there is a time when infants are not culpable before God to be an unwarranted hypothesis."[7]

Discussion of baptism elicited increased appreciation among Lutheran participants concerning the importance of the nurture of children and a renewed sense of challenge to take seriously mature responses of an articulated faith as the completion of baptism. It was also sensed that there was a movement away from "mere symbol" in the delegation. Baptism was seen as more than a token of loyalty by the obedient Christian. Lutherans affirmed a growing concern for a theology of childhood and the growing awareness of New Testament sacramentalism. There was also the fact that some Baptists are committed to the unrepeatability of baptism even if the proper norm is believers' baptism. (The recent Baptist–Lutheran Conversation in the Federal Republic of Germany was prompted in large part by the issue of rebaptism. Clarifications occurred without adequate resolution of the issue even though there was recognition of each other as churches.)[8]

B. Holy Communion

The Lutheran commitment to preserve both the objectivity of the sacraments as a means of grace and the necessity of faith for efficacious use of the sacraments was carried through also in the area of Holy Communion. The word of promise (institution) is of primary importance. The sacrament does not depend for validity upon personal worthiness. It is a means of grace that effects forgiveness and salvation for the believing sinner.

With respect to "presence" the Lutheran persuasion was presented that Christ is wholly present in his body and blood under signs of bread and wine, not by virtue of human power or the believer's faith. In dialogue Baptist statements inclined to assert more than a merely commemorative or figurative presence. Holy Communion was represented as an occasion for a heightened awareness of God's presence and power and therefore in these terms could be spoken of as a means of grace.

C. Church and Ministry

"Despite the divergences, however, we find profound bases for commonality and strong reason for recognizing each other's churches and ministry as authentic manifestations of the whole body of Christ."[9] In these words the dialogue recognized that there is an obvious common centering in Christ and the gospel. Stated agreements also indicated that the church is the body of Christ, not merely an association of like-minded people, and the church is made up of the justified who are incorporated by baptism into a visible community of faith.

III. Evaluation and Critique

One of the fruits of the dialogue was the not unexpected growth in mutual respect. The Baptist participants acknowledged explicitly the importance of the Lutheran heritage regarding grace, gospel, the priority of God, nurture, a corporate focus, and the ability to explicate actions theologically. Baptist contributions to a theology of the laity, a passion for mission and evangelism, the importance of the considered response to Jesus Christ, and highly nuanced involvement with the heart of American historical developments were noted by Lutheran participants. The general climate of the dialogue was congenial and was conducted on more than a superficial level. These comments reflected considered opinions that developed further during the course of the dialogues.

In this atmosphere some important successes occurred. (1) Most notably, a clear recognition developed of the need to have a twofold agenda, one on theology and one on the formative historical forces in the respective developments of these two movements. (2) There was a willingness to discover the direction of the encounter, giving integrity to the process in its own terms with several topics emerging from previous meetings. (3) Agreement was made on public statements which, while claiming only the authority of the participants, nonetheless serve in a modest way to begin the process of influencing a wider circle of theologically oriented persons in both communions. At the same time it is apparent from the formal statements that there are theological divergences which are both profound and tenacious. No easy resolution holding promise of altar and pulpit fellowship can be entertained as a prospect for immediately succeeding dialogues.

Any dialogue with another Christian tradition provides, of course, an opportunity for self-examination. The Baptist concern for the regenerate life can remind us of the importance of uniting God's deed in baptism with the concrete response of faith and faithfulness. The Lutheran concern to stress the graciousness of baptism does not deny that this sacrament is a convenantal act which calls forth a human response of faith. In exalting divine grace we have been tempted to turn the believer into a passive object, failing to recognize that grace is not known or affirmed apart from believing response. Baptists can remind us that grace is not contradicted by the fact that it seeks to covenant with us. Grace not only looks for a faithful response; our experience of grace actually excites a faithful response.

IV. Looking to the Future

In reviewing the results of this dialogue, one is impressed with a number of stubborn differences which call for rigorous theological and historical work.

1. On the theological front the unplumbed depths of differences regarding divine initiative and human response are suggestive of more rigid theological commitments than the dialogue articulated. Issues respecting faith, conversion, baptism and Communion, and the theology of the child and of nurture can be seen as having received only preliminary attention.

2. The second significant area is the deepened understanding of historical forces that is called for in ongoing discussions. This must occur both for the purpose of self-understanding as well as for understanding the other tradition. The "Americanization" of Lutheranism and the relation of Baptists to Anabaptists and to Arminianism and Calvinism are areas which were inadequately explored.

3. The process to date has taken the dialogue group to the edge of fundamental issues regarding grace and faith, which were dealt with primarily in terms of the different emphases from within each tradition. There did not appear to be an adequate vocabulary to arrive at decisive statements of differences sufficient to explain the distance between our communions. A continuing encounter could be the catalyst for further research and reflection on these themes.

4. Also of concern in the area of nontheological factors are the implications of the continuing "European character" of Lutheran identity and the interplay of Baptist development with American history and culture. This would necessarily constitute a major focus of a continued Lutheran–Baptist dialogue. The issue at stake is the issue of historical accident versus fundamental theological commitment.

A number of developments indicate the value and the method of continuing the Lutheran–Baptist dialogue:

1. Lutherans and Baptists are encountering each other geographically. The concentration of Lutherans in the Northeast and Midwest is shifting to the South. Simultaneously the national mission strategy of the Southern Baptist Convention brings the Baptist emphasis into areas of greater Lutheran concentration. This should be taken as an opportunity for constructive ecumenical encounter at all levels in the church.

2. Developments in "evangelical" and Baptist circles are narrowing the hermeneutical gap between the two churches, including a growing appreciation of critical and historical aspects of biblical research, a developing commitment to social responsibility, and increased ecumenical awareness and openness.

3. The appropriately modest goals for the conversations virtually guaranteed a sense and willingness to extend the process into the future. The introduction of the WCC document, *Baptism, Eucharist and Ministry*, could provide the catalyst for discovering some promising convergences in the dialogue between these two partners. The "process of reception" that is recommended for the church bodies in responding to BEM could well involve the continuation of this dialogue series focused on one of the controverted areas, namely, baptism.

4. In keeping with the obvious need to popularize conversations of this type, it was noted that further dialogues should involve laity with attention to broadening participation of women and minorities.

Finally, the modest goals set at the beginning in a sense guaranteed success even though it was a limited success. One might speculate that these modest goals were conditioned somewhat by the relatively successful history of dialogues with the sacramental-liturgical Roman Catholic and Episcopalian partners. Lutheranism in the American context has been rediscovering its identity with those of a more

"Catholic tradition," and ecumenism in the Protestant direction has therefore seemed to hold less promise or at least less interest. The affirmative dimensions of this dialogue, together with an appropriate Lutheran concern for the unity of the *entire* church, should inspire our efforts in both directions.

6

Lutheran–Evangelical/ Conservative Dialogue

Donald Huber
Edward Schroeder

The Lutheran–Conservative/Evangelical conversations (October 1979–April 1981) were not "bilateral dialogues" in the usual sense of the term. Rather, a series of four theological colloquia were held between certain Lutheran theology professors and certain Conservative/Evangelical seminary professors chosen by their seminary presidents in response to an invitation from LCUSA. Participants came from in and around Chicago, the site of the meetings. Thus neither group was "representative," although the Lutherans were appointed through official channels.

This information does not disparage the colloquia, but signals the first "given" of any attempt at bilateral dialogue with the kaleidoscopic Conservative/Evangelical tradition(s).

Conservative Evangelicalism, surely one of the most dynamic forces on the American scene today, takes on a different configuration when refracted through the prisms of Christian faith and life. Lutherans are generally aware that tensions exist with the Conservative/Evangelicals on the issues of baptism, the new birth, religious experience, church discipline, the meaning of the church, biblical authority, and the Christian calling in secular society. Admittedly both groups have internal disagreements on many of these items, yet there is a general Conservative/Evangelical perspective that is in tension with historic Lutheranism.

The Chicago colloquia recognized these traditional differences and addressed them head on. Some stereotypes dissolved and some mutual understandings arose, as is witnessed to by the proceedings.[1] From the "Declaration" produced by the participants we see that traditionally controverted topics stayed that way. The participants go on record with their consensus on "fidelity to the Gospel of the Lord Jesus Christ," on grace alone, faith alone, and Scripture alone. They also agree "that true evangelical faith expresses itself in discipleship marked by devotion to God and loving service to our neighbors." Where they had "not reached an understanding" was on scriptural authority, church and sacraments, and the ministerial offices.[2]

We believe that this accurately reflects the situation today between the two traditions. Participants from both sides of the table acknowledge that their different histories often shape their present perspectives and thus much remains to be done in the continuing conversations between the two. From the following observations we discern some contours of that remaining agenda:

1. Both traditions see themselves as movements within the church catholic and their particular accents as offered for the whole church's benefit. Yet the movements take on differing contours. The Lutheran movement is delineated by a particular historical period, the sixteenth century, and by authoritative confessional documents. The Conservative/Evangelical movement, however, is harder to define. It has no *Book of Concord,* no handful of dominant personalities who shaped the events of its history. Yet people in this movement sense their distinctive confessing tradition within the church as those who affirm, in the words of Donald Bloesch, the "centrality and cruciality" of Christ's work as declared in the Scriptures, the "necessity" for personal appropriation of Christ's work in one's own life, and the "urgency" for bringing this good news to a lost and dying world.[3]

2. Unclarity persists on how to relate "movement" to "denomination" in each group. Lutherans tend to expect that people in the Lutheran movement will be in Lutheran denominations. Yet few would deny that this same movement exists within other denominations as well, where, e.g., the "theology of the cross" undergirds faith and

practice. Evangelicals, on the other hand, take it for granted that their movement is transdenominational. Although some groups lay claim to the label "Conservative/Evangelical" for their denominational self-description, the evangelical movement is found throughout the main-line denominations. Thus when you encounter Lutherans, you expect them to be in a Lutheran church. When you bump into Evangelicals, they could be in almost any denomination.

3. In fact, Bloesch, in the work cited above, sees Lutherans as *a part of* evangelicalism. Thus he views the colloquia under discussion here as "all in the family." And indeed they do show a considerable degree of consensus, even to the point that controverted items within one of the movements have their parallel conflicts in the other. Yet it was hard to find consensus between the movements or even con-vergence at some points, especially in the area of sacramental theology and practice.

4. American Conservative Evangelicalism has exercised consid-erable influence on Lutheranism in America. Even today in Lutheran folk piety Billy Graham often shapes the Lutheran grass roots ethos much more than Luther's Catechisms do. It is not unusual for Lutheran seminarians to "return" to their Lutheran roots after coming alive to the faith via a detour through InterVarsity, Youth for Christ, or Campus Crusade. Therefore dialogue with this tradition does not belong on the Lutherans' back burner. The high public profile of Lutheran di-alogue with Roman Catholics, Episcopalians, and the Reformed over-shadows this grass roots datum. It is a bias that needs correcting.

Thus we urge the continuation of this dialogue as a high priority for Lutherans. Following are some possibilities for future agendas:

1. Mutual exploration of the "movement" motif. For us the ty-pology offered by Luther P. Gerlach and Virginia H. Hine, *People, Power, Change: Movements of Social Transformation*[4] proved helpful in clarifying the dynamics at work in both Lutheranism and Conser-vative/Evangelicalism. Other movement typologies might also prove beneficial.

2. Mutual exploration of parachurch structures and the "official" church. The parachurch structure so characteristic of Conservative/ Evangelicals throughout the world is not without significant parallels in American Lutheranism.

3. The pietist heritage in the past and the present of both movements.

4. An alternate approach to discussions of biblical authority. For example, subsequent dialogues might examine how Scripture is used

in specific situations, such as in ministry to the dying. Subsequent to such examination of Scripture in praxis would come historical hermeneutical theological reflection on such usage and its consequence for appropriating the faith.

5. Baptism, too, might be approached in a second round of dialogues initially as an issue of practice and pastoral ministry, with theological reflection following upon that.

If the dialogue is resumed, a crucial question is that of a *modus operandi*. We offer the following suggestions:

1. Expand the institutional context beyond that of seminaries. Lutherans tend to locate the teaching magisterium in the seminaries. Within the Evangelical tradition some of the most influential voices are not seminary professors, but editors, evangelists, Bible college teachers, and parachurch organization executives. Leaving them outside the conversations is unwise.

2. Promote dialogue at the grass roots. Although the point is a cliché on the ecumenical scene, it is still valid. Has American Lutheranism in its allergy toward "Fundamentalism" simply ignored a major segment of American Christianity in day-to-day ecumenism? It is true that some Conservative/Evangelicals seem not to be open to dialogue, but the same is true of some Lutherans. And *some* is not *all*. Many would and do respond favorably to sharing the faith with fellow believers in local ecumenical work and in parish-to-parish interaction.

In conclusion, we would underline the importance of listening carefully to the antiestablishmentarian, restitutionist stance of Conservative/Evangelicalism. As even the modest dialogue in 1979–81 demonstrates, the Conservative/Evangelical tradition has gifts to bring to Lutheranism. Historically this has been hard for Lutherans to acknowledge, but acknowledge it we must. Secondly, we would emphasize that it is doubtful that any "neat" outcome such as declarations of pulpit and altar fellowship is possible. The results of such a dialogue will probably be in intangible areas, such as a growing appreciation for the theological integrity of the respective traditions and perhaps movement toward theological consensus at certain points. Permit us to wonder aloud whether an activist, pragmatic American Lutheranism is prepared to engage in a process which is likely to produce few concrete results. We hope that it will.

7

Lutheran–Orthodox Dialogue

David Daniel
Daniel Martensen

Lutheran dialogue with the churches of the Orthodox East is qualitatively different from other bilateral efforts. Discussion of the method of proceeding with the conversations has been and still is central to the process, a fact reflected in the deliberations in 1978 of a meeting of Lutherans in Geneva preparing for world-level dialogue. The preparatory group reflected upon both the history of contacts between the two world communions since the sixteenth century and the extensive regional dialogue which has gone on since the 1950s primarily in continental Europe. Among their conclusions was this:

> It is clear that the Lutheran/Orthodox international dialogue requires that an evaluation if not a reconsideration of the methods used in the past bilateral conversations be undertaken. The critical evaluation of ecumenical methodology and structural approaches to dialogue should precede the dialogue as well as be carried out by the dialogue itself. It is not enough to compare statements of faith employing traditional tools of theological method. Ways must be found to fully integrate dimensions of spirituality and elements of linguistic differences into the dialogue experience. In many respects language as the most significant mode of human interaction with the world and other people gives shape to expressions of faith and style to worship. Without

sensitivity to these methodological and linguistic factors in the dialogue growth in mutual understanding will remain limited.

Regional and world-level dialogue has made it abundantly clear to Lutherans that in dialogue with the Orthodox we have to deal with expressions of the Christian life relatively unfamiliar to us. Two examples would be the centrality of the icon as a window to the divine in Orthodox spirituality and the all-important function of the Holy Liturgy (the celebration of which has cosmic significance for the Orthodox) as the context and instrument of the life of the church. These kinds of differences between the communions obviously require dialogue participants to develop new methods of ecumenical engagement.

Conversations involving Lutheran and Orthodox churches in the USSR, Rumania, Greece, the German Democratic Republic, the Federal Republic of Germany, Finland, Ethiopia, India, and the United States, to name just a few, have produced volumes of results. However, the evaluation of the quality and judiciousness of the theological findings contained in the results has just begun. It is clear that the evaluation of regional dialogue is linked to the self-understanding of the Lutheran churches involved and their relationship to the Lutheran world communion. The question of goals is also basic to the process of evaluating dialogue experience and results and basic to the process of making decisions about the method of dialogue.

Essentially, methodology has been the business of historians and sociologists, i.e., the *ex post facto* analysis of the way an event or dynamic happened. Behaviorists have pushed it in the direction of the future in attempting to determine what will happen. This last emphasis has been picked up in recent years by ecumenists. In ecumenical dialogue certainly any discussion of methodology presupposes some clarity about the goal involved. No doubt focusing on the goal can liberate dialogue participants from unproductive rehearsals of traditional theological argumentation. However, focusing primarily on the goal can also preclude creative breakthroughs and/or divine guidance. An appropriate methodology for Lutheran–Orthodox dialogue would have to reflect openness to the guidance of the Holy Spirit as well as the courage to reexamine the fundamental theological and ecclesiological presuppositions and expressions of the two communions.

The relationship between the setting of regional dialogue goals and the setting of goals for world-level dialogue is at the heart of the matter. Unofficial observations such as those in the following paragraph suggest the complexity of the relationship. In India dialogue participants tend to see unity as given. This experience of God-given unity and the press of the future give the ecumenical movement in India its character. In contrast, the fragile church–state relationship in the German Democratic Republic could be threatened by advocates of unity; in contexts where the churches' relationships to the government are constantly reviewed, international and national ecclesial agendas are shaped differently. No intention of union is expressed in the dialogue work of Finland. There is a feeling there that the world-level dialogue should not move too quickly and that it should deal with issues already considered in regional discussions. In Greece and in the Federal Republic of Germany it is clear that the change in postwar realities in Europe affect the dialogue process and its goals. At present there are 100,000 or more Orthodox migrant workers in the Federal Republic. In Ethiopia the primary goal of ecumenical dialogue is to "reduce the level of hatred." In pluralistic North America a goal may be to identify those components in our diversity which do not breach our understanding of the unity which is given; the current dialogue will report at the end of 1989. Lutheran–Orthodox dialogue in Rumania has been one of "faith and love." There social issues are dealt with consistently but with clearly defined limited objectives.

It is clear that the participants in the world-level dialogue at this point see their methodology characterized by integrity, openness, and adherence to a process rather than obedience to a preconceived blueprint for realizing unity.

The state of Lutheran–Orthodox dialogue does not lend itself to an evaluation which in any sense can be considered definitive, least of all an evaluation emerging from North America. However, a delineation of some challenges and tasks is certainly possible. Put in question form, such a catalogue would include the following:

1. What is the relationship between goal and approach in Lutheran–Orthodox dialogue?

2. How do Lutherans respond to the question posed by the Orthodox regarding the ecclesial character of world Lutheranism?
3. What symbolic acts of love and respect initiated by either or both communions at the local or regional level would properly enhance the dialogue?
4. How can the Lutheran–Orthodox conversation be catalytic and instructive for other bilateral dialogues, especially the Lutheran–Roman Catholic dialogue?
5. What unofficial middle-level ecumenical structures or programs might facilitate this bilateral?
6. How might this dialogue contribute to planning for the pan-Orthodox Council?
7. How can the dialogue process be used as a means for achieving intraconfessional consensus and cooperation?
8. How can worship and prayer life in the respective communions influence the dialogue process?

To say the least, Lutheran–Orthodox dialogue encourages Lutherans to do some fresh thinking about ecumenical questions and possibly even to pitch their tent in a new fashion in order to adjust to new ecumenical terrain.

PART TWO

A Thematic Analysis of the Dialogues

8

Justification

Carl E. Braaten

In this essay we will examine the ecumenical dialogues in which American Lutherans have been involved in light of two questions. The aim of the first one is purely descriptive: How was the topic of justification treated in the dialogue under consideration? The point of the second one is to make an evaluation: How adequately was the classical Lutheran interest in justification represented at the dialogue in question? In order to have a criterion by which to test whether the Lutheran concern has been well met, we are going to formulate the issue of justification from the point of view of Martin Chemnitz's *Examination of the Council of Trent.*[1] We have chosen Martin Chemnitz because he put the matter into a nutshell. He was a masterful and trustworthy expositor of the faith that moved the early adherents of the Augsburg Confession. Our limited intent is to identify what is at stake in the matter of justification and to ask whether Lutherans today continue to understand, appreciate, and hold themselves accountable to the essence of it.

Martin Chemnitz's Concern for the *Krinomenon*

Trent has accused and condemned Lutherans for teaching that believers receive only the forgiveness of sins and not the renewal of the Holy Spirit. Chemnitz replied that this is not the case. Lutherans do not neglect the renewal of the Spirit, nor do they take lightly the necessity of love, good works, and other virtues. Lutherans simply want to make clear that these things follow from justification as the absolution of sins and do not contribute to it. Others were counseling that the whole controversy between the Confessors and the Papalists was much ado about nothing, perhaps nothing but a difference of emphasis. Whereas the Lutherans typically emphasize justification as the *imputation* of the righteousness of Christ apprehended by faith, followed by renewal, love, and good works, the Papalists look upon justification in a more comprehensive manner as meaning the whole *process* of making sinners into righteous persons. Thus Lutherans supposedly are more narrowly concerned to stress the beginning of the process of actual salvation, whereas Catholics are more broadly concerned to include all aspects of the process in a balanced way. Neither side should need to deny the validity of the other's concerns. Perhaps they are both right. So goes the mediating counsel. Those who continue to insist on the basic differences are perhaps only satisfying "a morbid craving for controversy and for disputes about words."[2]

At this point Chemnitz points out that in this state of confusion and sophistry it is necessary to make a clean statement of the *krinomenon,* the chief point of difference in the controversy on the article of justification. He says that our concern is not to make trouble, to split the church, or to engage in scholastic abstractions. Our concern is rather for the truth of the gospel and the consolation of believers. What then is the chief point concerning justification?

We are faced with two different answers to the question of what has to happen to make us right with God. The question is: What has to come between the judgment of God and our sinfulness to bring about reconciliation? Both sides say that Christ has already come in between. The one side says that this is the gospel and this is enough to justify sinners before God. To let this be enough is what faith is all about. The other side says that this is only part of the gospel and therefore something more is needed, such as an inner renewal, a new obedience, and good works. In their favor is the fact, which Chemnitz acknowledges, that the word "justify" in the Bible is used in both senses, "to pronounce just" and "to make just." Counting up all the instances of the meaning of *dikaio, dikaios,* and *dikaiosyne* in the Bible can be an interesting word game, but

Chemnitz points out that what counts is how these words are used by Paul when he is explicitly addressing the question of how sinners are justified before God.

Chemnitz will not fudge at all on the real point at issue in the controversy. "There is simply nothing in man, whether he be Gentile or Jew, regenerate or unregenerate, by which he can be justified before God, that in this way the glory of justification may be truly attributed to Christ the Mediator alone, who has been apprehended by faith."[3] In other words, the issue is how we as sinners can stand before the judgment of God. Just at this point there is no room for even a tiny bit of consideration for the good works and virtues of the regenerate, which in their right place are indeed "very great and glorious."[4] What is at stake is the issue of eternal life. When we stand before the divine tribunal, we will let Christ plead our case as the divinely appointed defense attorney for sinners. Then we will not be judged on the basis of what is inherent in ourselves, for there is nothing there worthy enough that we may be justified. To speak of our good works as merits that might count for anything toward our justification before God is a kind of blasphemy. That we stand justified before God is due solely to the purely gratuitous grace, goodness, love, and mercy of the God who imputes the righteousness and merits of Christ to us.

The decrees of Trent, according to Chemnitz, deny that the justification of a sinner is *solely* the remission of sins, that people are righteous before God *solely* through the imputation of the righteousness of Christ, that they are justified *solely* by grace through the favor of God who forgives sins solely for Christ's sake. Contrariwise, the decrees of Trent affirm that the justification of the ungodly before God to life eternal is due not only to the remission of sins but also to the sanctification occurring in the inner life, so that such things as works of charity and morality count for something in a continuous process of salvation that proceeds beyond the grave until God is satisfied that there are enough credits to make up for the debits. The difference between these two models of justification is bound to be generative of vastly different types of ecclesial praxis.

Lutheran–Reformed Dialogues (USA)

The first dialogue in which Lutherans in America became involved was with the Reformed, initiated in 1962. The dialogue produced a "Summary Statement,"[5] which we will examine.

The summary begins with what the two traditions hold in common, affirming classical creedal truths about creation and redemption. It proceeds to acknowledge that with respect to law and gospel the two traditions provide a different emphasis. The Reformed tradition gives the law a wider and more positive scope, whereas the Lutheran phrase *lex semper accusat* is more restrictive than we find in Scripture and the tradition generally. The point, however, is questionable. The description of the law as "always accusing" in the Lutheran tradition (Ap 4:38; BC 112) is made in the context of a discussion of what counts for justification and the forgiveness of sins, and here the law has an accusatory function. This does not lead to antinomianism, for in other contexts the law is upheld in a positive light. The summary statement goes on to acknowledge disagreement on the relation of law and gospel in the Christian life. Calvinists have a major place for the law in the Christian life, while Lutherans are more reserved. In fact, it could have been brought out more candidly that Lutherans do not agree on the matter of the "third use of the law" and that this is a difference that goes beyond semantics.

In the sixth paragraph of the summary statement we find a direct word on justification. We must quote it in full: "We are agreed that the doctrine of justification by faith is fundamental in both traditions. We recognize, however, that for Lutherans this doctrine has played a more formative role in the articulation of theology. This difference is due in part to the historical situations in which Luther and Calvin did their theological work."[6] All of this is quite true, but the interesting question is "Why?" Why has this doctrine played a more formative role in Lutheranism? Is the answer to this question significant? Calvin and Luther worked in different historical situations, but there were Lutherans in Calvin's situation who did not agree with him. The historical situation often gets too much credit or blame for theological differences.

The summary statement ends by acknowledging that differences do exist between the Lutheran and Reformed traditions. The statement expresses gratitude to God for progress made in resolving their differences. What progress? What resolution? The statement leaves the impression that there are such, but offers no evidence to back it up. The participants acknowledge the need to resume the dialogue in the future.

The next dialogue we need to examine is the third one, entitled *An Invitation to Action: The Lutheran–Reformed Dialogue, Series III, 1981–83.* The second one, taking place in 1972–74, produced no published results until the final report was included in *An Invitation to Action* as part of the background for the report of the third series. In this series we are given a rather substantial joint statement on justification. The conclusion reads: "We agree that there are no substantive matters concerning justification that divide us." This statement goes far beyond the first series, which has concluded that differences do continue to exist. In this third dialogue the partners are bold to defend their conclusion with a number of arguments. First, they offer lengthy quotations from the Westminster Confession and the Heidelberg Catechism which provide very strong testimony to justification, as clear as we found in Chemnitz's *Examination.* Second, they adduce further evidence of confessional congruence, noting that during the Crypto-Calvinist controversy, 1560–74, justification was not an issue. Nor did Luther, Zwingli, Bucer, Melanchthon, and Oecolampadius disagree on justification at Marburg in 1529. Finally, we have the added weight of the Leuenberg Agreement affirming consensus on justification. All in all, Lutherans and Calvinists came to realize that never in their history has justification *per se* been an issue to divide the confessions. Never have they condemned each other on justification, plus there is now no need to revoke anathemas. As far as this issue is concerned, there is no reason why Lutheran and Reformed churches "should not at this time officially recognize and declare one another as churches in which the gospel is preached and taught."[7] Why did they refrain from using the word "rightly" or "purely"?

When we look at the bottom line of the Lutheran–Reformed dialogues on justification both in the U.S.A. and Europe, we must conclude that present-day Lutherans and Calvinists are not aware of any church-dividing issue on the topic of justification. It has not been so in the past, and there is no need to concoct one today. The Reformed side has spoken of justification in a way that Lutherans can affirm, but Lutherans must wonder why in all these dialogues the Calvinists have been totally silent about predestination and the decrees of the Synod of Dort. Is this part of the Calvinist tradition now a dead issue? Nowhere did the dialogues take up the issue of election and predestination. For Lutherans there is good news and consolation in the doctrine of election. It would have been useful for Lutherans and Calvinists to push their dialogue on justification to its very deepest dimension in the article on election. There is no explanation of why the dialogue stopped at the threshold of this issue. Surely there is unfinished business here.

We have noticed a remarkable shift from the first to the third series of dialogues, from the acknowledgment of disagreement between Lutherans and Calvinists to an outright claim of no basic difference on justification. However this shift is to be explained, that is the way matters stand today.

The Lutheran–United Methodist Bilateral Dialogue

The Lutheran–United Methodist bilateral consultation adopted a joint statement on baptism. The reference to justification is simple and terse. The introduction to the statement asserts: "We also share the biblical Reformation doctrine of justification by grace through faith. We are agreed that we are justified by the grace of God for Christ's sake, through faith alone and not by the works demanded of us by God's law." Then it goes on with a word about sanctification: "We also recognize the common emphasis on sanctification as a divinely promised consequence of justification."[8]

Our comment may be correspondingly brief. The classical *solas,* grace alone, Christ alone, faith alone, have been sparingly used. There is reference to "faith alone" apart from the works of the law, but a consensus statement for Lutherans could well afford to include the other *solas* as well, perhaps more relevant in our age of relativism and pluralism than in Luther's or Wesley's day. Approaching these documents with what Ricoeur calls a "hermeneutics of suspicion," one has to go behind the consensus statement into the background papers, and there one finds some important points. There is some discussion about whether Wesley held to the "exclusive particles" in the sense in which Lutherans have held them.[9] The major Lutheran papers in this dialogue are definitely aiming to transcend the usual distinctions between Lutherans and Methodists on soteriology, on the supposition that they need each other's strong points to compensate for each other's weak points, that there is room for legitimate pluralism, and that the church needs different ways of articulating the mystery of salvation. Thus we are told we need the Lutheran emphasis on orthodoxy, zeal for the truth of the gospel, as well as the Methodist concern for orthopraxis, commitment to holy living. One wonders about this. When you cross a Lutheran and a Methodist, you usually get a pietist, and Lutherans have produced their own share of these. However profoundly indebted we may be to our pietist forebears, we can not help but ask with respect to the teaching on justification whether pietism does not represent the beginning of its fall into the abysmal slough of subjectivism and moralism where the preaching of the gospel is now wallowing around in our churches. Are not the "exclusive particles" needed to keep the critical principle of justification from turning into spaghetti?

Lutheran–Conservative/Evangelical Dialogue

The Conservative/Evangelicals in this dialogue did not represent organized churches; they represented themselves as individuals and indirectly the religious movements with which they were affiliated. The dialogues focused on regeneration, justification, the nature of the church, and the authority of Scripture, the hottest issues over which the original splits from the established mother churches occurred. Needless to say, there was no real consensus, but the value of the process was affirmed by the participants.

The following paragraph aimed to locate a common core shared by evangelical Lutherans and Conservative/Evangelicals: "We acknowledge that salvation is by grace alone, through faith alone, and that those things which Christians believe are ultimately to be determined and tested by the standard of Scripture alone."[10] There is no mention of justification; the broader word "salvation" is used, thus avoiding the issue which the focus on justification raises. The one Lutheran background paper on justification was a mixed bag. Chemnitz's interest in a sharp statement of the *krinomenon* failed to come to expression probably because American Lutheranism is still mostly a product of the pietist reaction to Orthodoxy. Justification in its Pauline usage is a forensic metaphor. Why apologize for it? It brings out the truth that we have absolutely nothing of our own to interpose between the divine wrath and our sins unless we let Christ do for us what he alone is able to do, and that is to stand there in our place, as the one on whose account we are absolved from the sentence of condemnation, received into fellowship with God, adopted as God's children, and promised the gift of eternal life.[11]

Lutheran–Episcopal Dialogues

Lutherans and Episcopalians are now involved in their third series of dialogues, dealing with the church and its ministry. In the early seventies the first series issued a report dealing with Holy Scripture, Christian worship, baptism and confirmation, and apostolicity. Following the progress report, which claimed "growing consensus," recommendations were made. One of them called for recognition of agreement between Lutherans and Episcopalians on a number of fundamentals of church life and doctrine, among which was: "Justification by grace through faith as affirmed by both the Lutheran Confessions and the Anglican *Book of Common Prayer* and Thirty-Nine Articles of Religion." In the "Statement Addressed to Lutherans by the Lutheran Participants" there is no mention of justification.[12] There is no evidence that the article of justification played any role in the conversations. Nor did the matter of justification arise in the "Statement Addressed to Episcopalians."[13] The question of episcopacy loomed up as the really significant issue. It was conceded that Lutherans have the "apostolic gospel." All they lack is episcopal succession. Yet the Episcopalian statement penned by Reginald Fuller admits that Lutherans "have their reservations about our fidelity to the Gospel, as attested by the way we seem in their eyes to sit loose to the confessions of the Reformation. If we expect them to sympathize with our difficulties, we too must be ready to sympathize with theirs."[14] But these reservations that Lutherans allegedly have were not spelled out, nor what they might have to do specifically with justification.

The second series of the Lutheran–Episcopal Dialogue (LED II) issued a number of joint statements, and the first one (1978) was on justification. The others were on the gospel, the Eucharist, the authority of Scripture, and on apostolicity. Does the joint statement on justification meet the test of Chemnitz' *krinomenon?* It states: "At the time of the Reformation, Anglicans and Lutherans shared a common confession and understanding of God's justifying grace, i.e., that we are accounted righteous before God only for the merit of our Lord and Savior Jesus Christ, by faith, and not for our own works or deservings. The good news of salvation continues to comfort the people of God and to establish them in the hope and promise of eternal life." It goes on to state: "In the western cultural setting in which our communions, Episcopal and Lutheran, find themselves, the gospel of justification continues to address the needs of human beings alienated from a holy and gracious God." One more pertinent statement: "In both communions the understanding of the term 'salvation' has had different emphases. Among Lutherans, salvation has commonly been synonymous with the forgiveness of sins; among Episcopalians, salvation has commonly included not only the forgiveness of sins but also the call to and promise of sanctification. As we continue to listen to each other, may God grant that justification and the new life in the Spirit abound."[15]

There are many "salvation" words in the biblical tradition, as there are in the Lutheran tradition. The point of putting justification into its place of preeminent priority is not to crowd out all other biblical metaphors expressing the saving work of God through Christ and the Spirit. Lutherans also speak of the promise of sanctification and the new life in the Spirit, but they do not want to put the cart before the horse. Chemnitz referred to the sanctifying work of the Holy Spirit as "the second benefit of the Son of God." This must not be *identified* with the first benefit, nor *separated,* but properly *distinguished* from it for the sake of making clear that Christ alone stands as the reconciling mediator between the judgment of God and the alienation of sinners. The Lutheran concern was glossed over with imprecise language.

Lutheran–Baptist Conversation, 1979–81

These conversations produced common statements in three areas: divine initiative and human response; baptism and the theology of the child; and church and ministry. The statements about justification occur in a section entitled: "Common Understandings of Faith." Here are some of the statements:

"Lutherans and Baptists alike describe faith as being both a divine gift and a human response. Faith is made possible only by divine initiative, yet it is realized only through human response. In this human response it is recognized that the act of the human will in believing in itself is regarded as a work of God. It is the Father's drawing the sinner to himself; it is the work of the Holy Spirit in the life of the believer."[16] As the paragraphs unfold, it is clear that the intent of this common statement of faith is to stress both the divine agency in actualizing faith as well as the integrity of the human act of believing. "No one is able to believe without the prior work of God who frees a person from the bondage of sin and enables an unwilling person to do the will of Christ."[17] Faith is not an expression of the human potential; it is a gift of God. So there is no room for boasting. "True righteousness in us is accomplished by God's righteousness in Jesus Christ and is bestowed freely through faith in Christ."[18] All in all the statement is concerned to strike a balance between divine initiative and human response, using quite traditional language. Then where is the difference? The statement acknowledges that traditionally Lutherans have wanted to stress the divine side, whereas Baptists have tended to stress the human side. Lutherans veer to the objective ground of justification; Baptists tend to stress the subjective role of decision with regard to human faith. This difference works itself out consistently in their different positions on baptism, believer's baptism versus infant baptism.

There is something refreshingly candid about these conversations. It seems as though the lack of any pressure to bring about a reunification of their traditions has freed the participants to go at it with open recognition of both agreements and differences. More attention is paid to faith and justification in these conversations than we have seen heretofore.

Lutheran–Orthodox–Reformed Theological Conversation, 1973–75

These conversations dealt with "The Christian Gospel and Social Responsibility." The Report makes no mention of any discussion on justification. The only remark bordering on the theme states: "It is important for Lutherans to know that it is possible to articulate a Christian theology which is not based primarily on sin, forgiveness, and justification." [19] A new round of dialogues has commenced with the Orthodox. At the time of this writing the results of the most recent meetings between Lutherans and Orthodox, which reportedly deal with the contrast between justification and divinization, were not available.

Lutherans and Catholics in Dialogue 7

The seventh dialogue involving Lutherans and Catholics takes up the topic of "Justification by Faith," a topic as close to the heart of Lutheranism as the previous dialogue on papal infallibility is to Catholicism. Many commentators over the years have expressed surprise that a subject so foundational for Lutheran identity would be placed only seventh on the agenda, the previous six being more specifically of high priority for Catholics, such as dogma, sacrifice, ministry, papal primacy, and infallibility. Looking back over the dialogues, one could plausibly conclude that the Catholic side set the agenda and the Lutherans were invited to play ball on Catholic grounds. This impression was reinforced by the announcement that the present round would take up the cult of the saints and Mary.

The dialogue on justification was concluded with press reports that Lutherans and Catholics have reached "a fundamental consensus on the gospel," [20] although they admitted that even after five years of dialogue they still had differences and that "some of the consequences of the different outlooks seem irreconcilable, especially in reference to particular applications of justification by faith as a criterion of all church proclamation and practice." [21] What sense does it make to say that they share a fundamental consensus on the gospel but still hold irreconcilable differences on justification, particularly in light of the Lutheran insistence that justification by faith alone is the "article by which the church shall stand or fall?" It seems that there are two currents of thought running through this document, one claiming convergence bordering on consensus, the other admitting continuing tension and difference. At one place the idea of complementarity was suggested, namely, that both traditions,

precisely in their opposition, are not contradictory, but complementary.[22] Each side takes its turn in saying to the other, "Yes,
but. . . ." "You are right, but here is the other side of the coin!"
But is this theory of complementarity really viable? May it not be
equally plausible that we have two different coins glued together?
That is what Martin Luther thought and that is what Martin Chemnitz
taught. Maybe they were only looking at one side of the coin, or
maybe they found some coin of another realm circulating in the
church.

Let us take a look at some paragraphs.

In paragraph 118 it is stated that "Catholics, on their side, are
wary of using any one doctrine as the absolute principle by which
to purify from outside, so to speak, the Catholic heritage." According to the Reformers the article of justification does not come
from *outside* the Catholic heritage; it lies within the soil of the
biblical gospel from which the church lives and by which it is
corrected. It does not come from outside except in the sense that
the gospel is always *beyond* the human powers of mind and will
and feelings to conceive or create or generate. This radical assess-
ment of the human condition, such as we find in Luther's *Bondage
of the Will,* is not one side of the coin; it is the truth concerning the
human condition *coram deo.*

In paragraph 132 it is stated that the idea of salvation in Paul is
conveyed through an abundance of images, such as expiation, redemption, reconciliation, adoption, sanctification, and the like, but
that "righteousness/justification is the primary way the apostle describes what God has done for us in Christ." Then it concludes:
"Though sometimes intertwined with righteousness/justification,
these images point to dimensions of God's saving activity that cannot
easily be denoted by forensic terminology, even though the forensic
emphasis *may be needed* for their proper interpretation" (emphasis
added). What is conveyed by allowing that the "forensic emphasis
may be needed" in the church? This is like saying that Luther *may*
have had a point, Lutherans may have something to contribute to
the total picture of complementary truths. How about saying "is
needed"?

In paragraph 152 it is stated: "What has emerged from the present
study is a convergence (though no uniformity) on justification by

faith considered in and of itself, and a significant though lesser convergence on the applications of the doctrine as a criterion of authenticity for the church's proclamation and practice." Then in subsequent paragraphs it proceeds to explain and qualify these assertions. Having asserted that there is material convergence, in paragraph 154 it offers evidence to the contrary, stating that: "The Lutheran hermeneutical understanding of justification (paragraphs 88–93) in some ways heightens the tension with Catholic positions. It does so by excluding from the gospel proclamation all reference to the freedom and goodness of fallen human beings on the grounds that this would undermine the unconditionality of God's promises in Christ. Such interpretation raises even more questions from Lutherans regarding Catholic descriptions of justification as a process of ontological transformation." Here we are getting into the nittygritty of the issue of what Martin Chemnitz called the *krinomenon*, the chief point of difference between Lutherans and Trent. But this paragraph evades the point in controversy by attributing the difficulty to different structures of thought. This is clearly an evasion of the issue. Through historical study and imagination it is possible for scholars to learn more than one language and more than one system of conceptuality. It is possible to discern incompatible meanings under the conditions of a plurality of thought structures.

We would question whether the Lutheran hermeneutical position excludes "all reference to the freedom and goodness of fallen human beings." Not at all. Even Luther clearly stressed that there is freedom and goodness in certain *coram*-relationships, not *coram deo,* to be sure, but most certainly *coram mundo, coram hominibus,* and *coram meipso.* But these horizontal coram-relationships are not potentially productive of a change for the better *coram deo.* A great deal of misunderstanding of the Lutheran position has arisen both among Lutherans and others because of a failure to make the proper distinctions.

Paragraph 157 reiterates the agreement stated in paragraph 4, namely: "Our entire hope of justification and salvation rests on Christ Jesus and on the gospel whereby the good news of God's merciful action in Christ is made known; we do not place our trust in anything other than God's promise and saving work in Christ." This is a fine statement, but it is followed by another. "Such an affirmation is not fully equivalent to the Reformation teaching on justification according to which God accepts sinners as righteous for Christ's sake on the basis of faith alone." Here we have the problem. The first statement sounds equivalent to the second in Lutheran ears, but we are told it is not, because Catholics find it susceptible of an interpretation whereby justification is a process of gradual inward transformation on the way to final salvation.

Since we wrote the above reaction to the seventh dialogue, the background papers, previously unavailable, have been published. They do not as a whole bear out the claim of having reached a "fundamental consensus on the gospel." One statement by Carl Peter reinforces Martin Chemnitz's interpretation: "Trent spoke guardedly but did endorse human cooperation with God's grace in the process of leading to justification."[23] There is no need to review all these background papers. Nowhere do the Catholic participants yield on the chief point that for them justification is something that happens at the end of a conversion process and that it involves not merely the divine acceptance through the forgiveness of sins, but also sanctification of the inner life through a voluntary cooperation with the grace of God.

9

Baptism

Timothy F. Lull

I. Context and Criteria

Baptism has often been considered *the* ecumenically uniting doctrine, and it is easy to see why this has been the case. Except for the disagreement with the Anabaptists at the time of the Reformation, there was less division about this topic in the West than about the Eucharist or ministry or justification or authority in the church. And according to the methods of biblical study in our time, a topic like baptism lends itself well to common, interconfessional work.

Thus the general pattern of recent dialogues has been not to consider baptism so often or at such great length as some of the other doctrines. The exception would be in dialogues with Baptist groups or in cases where a "manageable" topic was desired at an early stage of discussion.

The thesis of this essay is that it is a mistake to conclude so quickly that there are no major differences among the churches regarding baptism. In fact, the theological climate since the Reformation has changed in such a direction that much of what the Reformation taught (and Lutherans still assume) about baptism has been under attack for the past 150 years.

This is especially the case for certain strands of Protestant theology that have come out of state–church situations in Europe. In the past century and a half there has been a progressive loss of confidence in the way of teaching about baptism that was widely assumed by several traditions at the time of the Reformation.

The attack on baptism, especially infant baptism, in this form traces back to Kierkegaard, although he did not become an international theological influence until the early part of this century. It was picked up and popularized by Karl Barth, first in his lecture, "The Teaching of the Church Regarding Baptism" (1943),[1] and then in the fragment, *Church Dogmatics* 4,4 (1967).[2] The current major critic of baptismal theology and practice stemming from the Reformation is Jürgen Moltmann, especially in his *Church in the Power of the Spirit* (1975).[3] A certain form of this attack has also been found in the writings of Robert Jenson, especially *Visible Words* (1978),[4] although it may be that the source for Jenson is as much his love for the pattern of Eastern Christianity as influence from Barth.

But all of these theologians hold a common view that the baptismal practice of the West has been one of indiscriminate infant baptism. They argue that under the guise of a theology of grace, the churches of Europe (and North America?) have actually found a way to maintain Christendom even though the level of commitment and sincerity of the promises was stretched to the breaking point. Most of them—especially Moltmann—seem to envision a church reformed in a "sectarian" direction.

Therefore it is extremely appropriate to look at the dialogues and documents about baptism and to look at them with more care than has sometimes been taken when the assumption has been that all will surely agree here (except the Baptists). But how can we know what to hope for from a Lutheran theological perspective?

One checklist of six Lutheran concerns can be generated from the Augsburg Confession and the Small Catechism:

1. Original Sin and the Need for Baptism
It is also taught among us that since the fall of Adam all men who are born according to the course of nature are conceived and born in sin. That is, all men are full of evil lust and inclinations from their mothers' wombs and are unable by nature to have true fear of God and true faith in God. Moreover, this inborn sickness and hereditary sin is truly sin and condemns to the eternal wrath of God all those who are not born again through Baptism and the Holy Spirit.

Augsburg Confession, Article 2 (BC 29)

2. Baptism as a Sacrament—God's Word
Baptism is not merely water, but it is water used according to God's command and connected with God's Word.

Small Catechism, Part 4 (BC 348)

3. Baptism as Salvation
It effects forgiveness of sins, delivers from death and the devil, and grants eternal salvation. . . .

Small Catechism, Part 4 (BC 348–49)

4. Baptism Founded in Grace—Received in Faith
It is not the water that produces these effects, but the Word of God connected with the water, and our faith which relies on the Word of God connected with the water. For without the Word of God the water is merely water and no Baptism. But when connected with the Word of God it is a Baptism, that is, a gracious water of life and a washing of regeneration in the Holy Spirit,. . .

Small Catechism, Part 4 (BC 349)

5. Baptism as the Foundation for Life in the World
. . . the new man should come forth daily and rise up, cleansed and righteous, to live forever in God's presence.

Small Catechism, Part 4 (BC 349)

6. The Appropriateness of Infant Baptism
It is taught among us that Baptism is necessary and that grace is offered through it. Children too, should be baptized, for in Baptism they are committed to God and become acceptable to him.

Augsburg Confession, Article 9 (BC 33)

Lutherans may well have other concerns, even on the basis of the Confessions. And some of these points may require a certain reformulation today to be understood rightly. But this list will begin to give a picture of the relative adequacy of any statement from the theological vision of baptism in Lutheran theology.

II. Lutheran–Roman Catholic Dialogue on Baptism

The Lutheran–Roman Catholic Dialogue in the United States took up "One Baptism for the Remission of Sins" as its second topic. In light of the very real success of the first discussion of the Nicene

Creed, this too seemed a promising topic. It was considered at a meeting in February 1966.

Unlike all subsequent dialogues in this series, the group issued no common statement. They were content to let two participants, Warren Quanbeck for the Lutherans and Msgr. Joseph Baker for the Roman Catholics, summarize the achievement of the four-day meeting. The published results also include some very fine papers,[5] but the summary statements cannot be considered to have the same authority or focus as an agreed common statement. There is a very brief statement at the end asserting:

> We were reasonably certain that the teachings of our respective traditions regarding baptism are in substantial agreement, and this opinion has been confirmed at this meeting.[6]

Thus for a more detailed picture of the reason for such confidence in agreement, one must go to Quanbeck's summary narrative.

Neither Quanbeck nor Baker provides sufficient evidence to review the checklist in Part I, but it seems clear that most of these themes were covered. Original sin was a major topic of discussion and a source of difficulty to many participants from both churches.

> At least in its popular expositions it is too individualistic and inadequately personal to do justice to the scriptural teaching.[7]

But it does not appear that there was a desire on either side to reject original sin and the necessity of baptism as much as a desire for an appropriate contemporary formulation.

In terms of baptism as a divine word and as salvation, the Quanbeck report seems to indicate that a recovery of biblical eschatology seemed to enhance and clarify both of those aspects of baptism.[8] There was mutual admission that some historical arguments for infant baptism seem to have been overstated, but no inclination apparent to abandon or greatly curtail this practice.

"A sharp difference in ways of theological thinking" emerged in regard to penance and forgiveness. Roman Catholic talk of "human collaboration with God," even though carefully linked to grace, struck Lutherans as dangerous and prefigured many of the difficult points in the recent seventh series on "Justification by Faith." And this also has clear implications for a difference in ethics. Both would see the Christian life founded in baptism, but Lutherans have stressed the need for daily return to baptism in contrast to a Catholic stress on hope for transformation.[9]

It is difficult to reconstruct the entire four days of dialogue, but the conclusion of "substantial agreement" does not seem farfetched. On the other hand, differences of emphasis within the teaching regarding baptism itself, though perhaps not incompatible, foreshadow much deeper difficulties which emerge fully in a discussion of the fruit of baptism in the life of Christians.

III. Lutheran–Methodist Dialogue on Baptism

A second major discussion of baptism is found in the Lutheran–Methodist U.S. Dialogue, which took place in the years 1977–79 and which issued a common statement on December 11, 1979. It is a thorough and careful statement which allows the theological evaluator to raise many questions, and the statement is accompanied by a number of fine supporting papers.[10]

Some of the Lutheran concerns receive strong and explicit affirmation in the statement. Baptism is a sacrament, a means of grace (#2). In baptism the Holy Spirit gives new birth, forgiveness, and participation "in the new age initiated by the saving act of God in Jesus Christ" (#9). Infant baptism is appropriate because "the divine invitation obligates all believers to be baptized" and because "no person should be excluded from Baptism for reasons of age or mental capacity" (#7 and #8).

But three other matters are more questionable. There is no direct mention of original sin; it is the command of God alone that seems to make baptism an urgent matter rather than something dangerous or precarious in the human situation without God.

The relation between grace and faith is stated very carefully, and a strong affirmation of justification is included.[11] But the statement goes on to affirm a "common emphasis on sanctification as a divinely promised consequence of justification" that would certainly need further elaboration to satisfy many Lutherans (#2).

That is especially the case because later in the statement a potentially glowing picture of the ethical transformation wrought by baptism is presented:

> Baptism looks toward a growth into the measure of the stature of the fullness of Christ (Eph. 4:13). By this growth, baptized believers should manifest to the world the new race of a redeemed humanity which puts an end to all human estrangement based, for example, on race, sex, age, class, nationality, and disabling conditions. (#11)

These hopes for the world are not necessarily incompatible with Lutheran theology, but greater clarity would be needed as to how they are seen to flow from baptism and to explain the fact that they are not so clearly the marks of the baptized in the world as we know it.

It would be difficult to prove that this dialogue represents a lesser degree of agreement on baptism than that achieved by the Lutheran–Roman Catholic dialogue. If there is avoidance of original sin here, there is greater willingness to embrace radical language about justification. But both Catholics and Methodists seem willing to claim for baptism an expectation of transformation of the person and community that Lutherans have usually opposed.[12]

IV. Lutheran–Baptist Dialogue on Baptism

In the same period when Lutherans and Methodists were having their discussion of baptism (1977–79), an important dialogue was begun between Lutheran and Baptist churches in North America. In 1981 three common statements were accepted, "Divine Initiative and Human Response," "Baptism and the Theology of the Child," and "Church and Ministry." Because of obvious historical differences, this group had an especially challenging assignment.

About what then could they agree, especially in reference to our checklist of six Lutheran concerns? There was a common admission of the difficulty in expressing the right relation between divine initiative and human response. Nevertheless, both churches wanted to insist that "Faith is made possible only by the divine initiative" and "to avoid the implication that the act of believing is made possible by an innate human power."[13]

But this common concern developed in quite different directions for a variety of reasons, especially because of different concepts of the church.

> Baptists see believer's baptism as most consonant with the concept of a regenerate church. Baptism is understood primarily as a sign of the gospel and the believer's response to it. It publicly attests the redemptive deed of God in Christ and the baptized person's trust in Christ as Savior, identification with him in his death and resurrection, and confession of him as Lord. Since faith involves a conscious, informed, voluntary decision, and baptism is an act of obedience in following Christ as Lord and Savior, an infant is considered to be incapable of such an act and is, therefore, not a proper candidate for baptism. Baptists understand the scriptural order to be: repent, believe, and be baptized. For Baptists, personal faith on the part of the candidate is therefore a prerequisite for the administration of baptism.[14]

Here we see real differences from the Lutheran concerns clearly and sharply acknowledged. This is also found, for example, in the discussion of "Baptism and the Theology of the Child," the second common statement. Sharp differences between the traditions are acknowledged in regard to original sin, with Baptists unable to accept the possibility of infant faith, but Lutherans "regard the idea that there is a time when infants are not culpable before God to be an unwarranted hypothesis."[15]

Other important differences in ecclesiology are discussed in the third common statement on "Church and Ministry." A central one is the concept of baptism as means of grace for Lutherans and as divine ordinance for Baptists. These differences are not surprising and the sharpness and charity with which they are expressed are admirable. It is clear that there is only minimal agreement between these churches. But that will be an interesting issue to reconsider when we come in the next section to consider *Baptism, Eucharist and Ministry*, in which Lutherans and Baptists both participated.[16]

V. Baptism in Wider Ecumenical Statements

The most extensive discussion of baptism in recent years was generated by the *Baptism, Eucharist and Ministry* statement of the

Faith and Order Commission of the World Council of Churches. In this statement theologians from the wide group of traditions represented in Faith and Order (WCC member churches and Roman Catholics) tried to produce a substantial common statement on these very difficult and divisive ecumenical topics.

A statement commonly made by Lutherans is: "Keep your eye on *ministry;* that's where the tricks are. After all, what could we worry about in baptism except infant vs. believer's baptism?" But given some of the diversity concerning baptism that we have seen in the dialogues above, it makes sense to raise the same Lutheran concerns in regard to the baptism portion of Faith and Order Paper 111.

If we begin with the Western church's teaching of original sin and the seriousness of the need for baptism, it has to be said that there is scarcely a trace of that in the statement and for good reasons. The Orthodox were eager to see that the common statement not follow the Augustinian theology of the West. Theologically liberal churches find the doctrine of original sin archaic and past reformulation. Politically liberationist churches fear the doctrine of original sin provides easy grounds for explaining and even justifying the injustice in the world.

In fact, the statement makes the same kinds of startling claims for what baptism accomplishes ethically that were found in the Methodist–Lutheran Dialogue discussed in Chapter 4 of this book.

> Thus those baptized are pardoned, cleansed, and sanctified by Christ, and are given as part of their baptismal experience a new ethical orientation under the guidance of the Holy Spirit.[17]

But while these strong claims are made for what baptism does, it is less clear that baptism is regeneration in the sense that the Augsburg Confession discusses; if in BEM the ethical transformation is very great, the claim on eternal salvation for the baptized person is very tentative. Those who are baptized are "free," but that freedom is for life "here and now." Even more important is the conditional nature of what is promised unless faith follows; "the necessity of faith for the reception of the salvation embodied and set forth in baptism is acknowledged by all churches."[18]

This might be understood in a way compatible with Lutheran teaching, especially were it more closely linked with the acknowledgment that "the life of the Christian is necessarily one of continuing struggle yet also of continuing experience of grace."[19] But the greatest stress here seems to be on the transformation that must follow baptism.

As they grow in the Christian life of faith, baptized believers demonstrate that humanity can be regenerated and liberated. They have a common responsibility, here and now, to bear witness together to the gospel of Christ, the Liberator of all human beings.[20]

The distance of these views from the Lutheran concerns for baptism seems very great and not at all surprising, given the cumulative picture of differences which has emerged throughout the dialogues considered in this paper and the representation of all these groups and others in the Faith and Order Movement.

But it would also be necessary to mention that while the document allows infant baptism, it does this in a grudging way, giving the clear impression (following Barth and Moltmann) that indiscriminate infant baptism is the major danger in regard to baptismal practice today.[21] True as this may be in some places, there is no recognition that overly discriminate adult baptism (especially when linked to the notion of a "true, gathered church") can be equally dangerous for the gospel. Some Baptist-type churches in North America have shown themselves to be quite as capable of being culturally captive as those churches which stand in the main Constantinian tradition.

The thrust of the document seems to be ethical and liturgical. It seems to assert that believers' baptism and infant baptism are both adequate and no barrier to closer communion. This runs the danger of rushing past certain deeper differences related to infant baptism which seem more adequately and honestly faced in the Lutheran–Baptist dialogue.

Responses of the Lutheran Church in America and of The American Lutheran Church have detailed some of these inadequacies rather carefully. The LCA response calls for a "clearer expression of the dynamic of sin and grace." The ALC document is somewhat more critical of the Lima text, complaining about both the tendency to see baptism as "a rite of commitment" and about oversimplicity in the discussion of believers' and infant baptism.[22]

A report of one section of the Budapest Assembly of the LWF also complains of the treatment of infant baptism in BEM.

> To put believers' baptism and infant baptism on a par makes it appear that it does not matter which is used. The understanding of "faith" in relationship to the *promissio Dei* does not reflect the Lutheran tradition. The document does not stress baptism as solely God's saving act.[23]

What can be said about the consensus on baptism in the Faith and Order Statement? It seems far less than in the Lutheran–Roman Catholic or Lutheran–Methodist dialogues discussed above. It seems that most of the traditional Lutheran concerns, except perhaps that of baptism as a sacrament, are ignored or slighted.

VI. A Personal Conclusion

The evidence may strike others in a different way. But it seems to me that the traditional Lutheran view of baptism is not only part of our heritage, but a powerful way of understanding the gospel rooted in grace and received in faith. It is a very different voice from that sounding in many churches today. Lutherans ought to hold on to some of these emphases, not simply from loyalty to the past but also for the sake of theological diversity in the church catholic.

This is not to suggest that Lutherans have nothing to learn from others or that scriptural and historical studies have not put a number of difficult questions before us. But I wonder who else will be willing to fight hard for a doctrine of baptism strongly emphasizing the grace of God when almost every other church has some kind of transformation in mind for the world (personal or social) that baptism must generate. Moreover, Lutherans will have to state their concern sharply and passionately if they are to be heard as doing something more than being predictably Lutheran in preferring one thing to another.

The problem of ethics and of suffering in the world is a serious one, but a human-centered, optimistic theology of baptism does not seem to me the only way to confront injustice in the world today. It is more likely to turn the church into a group of those who share the same ethical vision.

In fact, I think more and "harder" discussion of baptism with all our dialogue partners would yield a better and more consistent picture of our various relationships and theological passions. It would be interesting to get the Episcopalians and the Reformed (as well as the Methodists) to discuss with us the very ambiguous statement regarding baptism in *The COCU Consensus:*

> Baptism in the case of adults is the enactment of a personal decision of faith, repentance, and loving obedience, which is a response in the power of the Spirit to the gracious call of God in Christ. In the case of infants it is the act by which the child of a Christian family is sacramentally placed within the sphere of God's grace and the church's pastoral nurture, with a view to being taught and led to a subsequent act of personal faith in Christ.[24]

Is that last sentence (without qualification) possible for those who agree with us in any very deep way about the gospel and how God's grace comes to us in baptism? It may be that we have been passing over baptism too quickly, assuming that we agree, only to find subtle points that were ignored not so subtle when we come to major differences on justification, ethics, and the church.

10

Eucharist

Edward Schroeder

"We want to remind our readers of the real issue," says Melanchthon in Apology 24:10 on the Mass. "Both parties . . . must deal only with the point at issue and not wander off into side issues, like wrestlers fighting for their position. In the same way our opponents should be forced to discuss the point at issue. Once the real issue of the controversy is clear, it will be easy to evaluate the arguments both sides have presented" (BC 251).

And what was that "point at issue" in the Lutheran–Roman Catholic dialogue of 1530–31?

That the Lord's Supper does not grant grace *ex opere operato* and does not merit for others, whether living or dead, forgiveness of sins or of guilt or of punishment *ex opere operato*. This position is established and proved by the impossibility of our obtaining the forgiveness of sins *ex opere operato* through our works and by the necessity of faith to conquer the terrors of sins and death and to comfort our hearts with the knowledge of Christ; for his sake we are forgiven, his merits and righteousness are bestowed upon us. "Since we are justified by faith, we have peace" (Rom. 5:1). This is so firm and sure that it can prevail against all the gates of hell. (Ap 24:11; BC 251)

What is the "point at issue" in today's Lutheran bilateral dialogues regarding the Lord's Supper? It is not the point at issue that agitated Melanchthon. That is a defect that brings no credit to the Lutheran dialogues. Whether it is, by contrast, "wrestlers fighting for *their* position" remains to be seen. Data on the Lord's Supper in the bilaterals are found only in the Lutherans' conversations with Episcopalians, Roman Catholics, and the Reformed. All the other dialogues are mute on the subject.

Dialogue with the Episcopalians

The Data

The first major publication from the first Lutheran–Episcopal dialogue (LED 1) produced no explicit document on the Lord's Supper beyond the "Summary Statements Derived from the First Four Dialogues":

> 1. We agree that the proclamation of the Gospel and the celebration of the Holy Eucharist constitute the distinctive and central act of Christian worship. We discovered, however, that more attention should be given to precisely what the Eucharist means and how it is to be celebrated.
> 2. In viewing our several Eucharistic traditions in perspective, we agreed that unity in Eucharistic practice is to be found more in the "shape" of Eucharistic liturgies than in fixed texts.
> 3. We agreed that further discussion as to just what is meant and not meant by the phrase "Eucharistic Sacrifice" would be generally helpful. [Then come bibliographic references to *Lambeth 1958* and L–RC 3 *Eucharist as Sacrifice*.]
> 4. We agreed that some measure of pulpit and altar fellowship between our communions is desirable.[1]

The LED 1 volume concludes by including the full text of the Pullach report from the international LED (1972). That report has three paragraphs on the Lord's Supper. Paragraph 67 says that the church obediently performs the acts commanded by Christ and "receives in this way the body and blood of Christ, crucified and risen, and in him the forgiveness of sins and all other benefits of his passion." In paragraph 68 "both communions affirm the real presence of Christ, but neither seeks to define precisely how this happens," and in paragraph 69:

> Both traditions affirm that Christ's sacrifice was offered once and for all for the sin of the world. Yet without denying this fundamental

truth both would recognize that the Eucharist in some sense involves sacrifice. In it we offer our praise and thanksgiving, ourselves and all that we are, and make before God the memorial of Christ's sacrifice. Christ's redemptive act becomes present for our participation. Many Anglicans and some Lutherans believe that in the Eucharist the church's offering of itself is caught up into his one offering. Other Anglicans and many Lutherans do not employ the concept of sacrifice in this way.[2]

LED 2 produced a "Joint Statement on Eucharistic Presence," but nothing on Eucharist as sacrifice. Its six paragraphs say:

1. There are similarities and differences in the Reformation and early post-Reformation eucharistic theologies of Lutherans and Anglicans. Regarding "presence" the Anglicans "followed the Reformed emphasis on the spiritual eating by faith, thus denying that . . . unbelievers partake of Christ." In more recent times there is a "growing convergence on the essentials of eucharistic faith and practice."

2. The eucharistic celebration of word and sacrament is the heart and center of the life and mission of the church as the body of Christ in and for the world.

3. Christ's presence is proclaimed in a variety of ways in the eucharistic liturgy. "It is the risen Christ himself who presides at each assembly of his people . . . who is represented in a special way by the ordained ministers . . . who gives himself in his body and blood as both our sacrifice and our feast."

4. "The Church's celebration rests upon the Word and authority of Christ, who commanded his disciples to remember him in this way until his return. According to his word of promise, Christ's very body broken on the cross and his very blood shed for the forgiveness of our sins are present, distributed and received, as . . . fruits of that atoning sacrifice. . . . It is not our faith that effects this presence of our Lord, but by the faith we have received, the blessings of the Lord . . . are sealed to us until he comes. . . ."

5. This encounter with the Lord enables and empowers his people to be the body of Christ in and for the world. Therefore frequent congregational celebration is commended (including the sick and homebound) along with the "true use of the sacrament [viz.,] . . .

to eat and drink the body and blood in the faith that our Lord's words give what they promise."

6. "In recent years, through biblical scholarship, there has been a growing appreciation of the eschatological dimension of the Lord's Supper." Therefore the proleptic "unity of the Church in Christ here and now . . . is to be sought wherever sufficient agreement can be reached."[3]

In the 1982 Helsinki report of the Anglican–Lutheran European Commission, the core assertions of Pullach (1972) are reaffirmed, garnished with flavors from the herbarium of BEM: *anamnesis*, the kingdom, pneumatology, and service to the world.

Comment

Except for the proleptic dispute between Henry VIII and Luther there has, to my knowledge, been no tradition of Lutheran–Episcopal debate (agreement or disagreement) on the Lord's Supper. Thus the participants in this dialogue were analogous to characters in search of a playwright. It appears that the "script" they chose was in some sense "borrowed," the "presence" question from the Reformed–Lutheran side of things and the "sacrifice" item from the Roman–Lutheran side. Or was this the natural spinoff of a Protestant–Episcopal (Geneva-Rome) matrix that is at the center of the Episcopal ethos? If that is even half true, it might offer Lutherans a way to pursue, *à la* Melanchthon, the "real issue" behind the "side issues" of presence and sacrifice. For there does not seem to be any real issue in the LED materials. The reader cannot escape a sense of "ho hum" in, with, and under the LED statements from both sides of the Atlantic.

The sixteenth century sacramental issue *re* sacrifice was the *sola fide* issue, says Melanchthon, the never ending debate about "faith alone." A generation later the Formula of Concord saw the same *sola fide* to be "the point of issue" in the new controversy with the Sacramentarians on the topic of Christ's presence in the Supper. Lutherans in twentieth-century dialogues cannot afford to ignore such a "real issue" when discussing these other sacramental issues today. Yet it seems that they did in the LED, thus corroborating Reumann's observation that both in biblical study and in ecumenical dialogue on the Lord's Supper nowadays "the tendencies in recent years have probably been more in the direction of eucharistic objectivization than in a stress upon faith."[4]

That is clearly the case in LED. Are the Lutherans in the next two bilaterals any different, those in dialogue with the Reformed and with the Roman Catholics? Will they too reinforce the Reumann rule of thumb?

Dialogue with the Roman Catholics

The Data

The publication *Facing Unity* (1985) from the Roman Catholic–Lutheran Joint Commission describes the present status this way in paragraph 76:

> A great deal of progress towards a common understanding and celebration of the *eucharist* has been made in recent years as a result of numerous dialogues between our churches at various levels. In the course of these dialogues it proved possible to reconcile positions with regard to the understanding of the eucharist that had previously been thought to be in conflict and were therefore seen as divisive (sacrifice of the Mass, eucharistic presence); many of the remaining differences are within the common sphere, thus depriving them of their divisive force. Regarding liturgical form, both churches are moving towards growing consensus in the basic elements of eucharistic celebration.[5]

The detailed agreements on presence and sacrifice referred to by the L–RC Joint Commission were the product of the U.S.A. LC–RC dialogue. L–RC 3 (1967) is the document on this. In the concluding statement on the "growing consensus" they say that these two issues dominated their agenda. On *sacrifice* they enunciate two agreements never denied by either confession and four items of past divergences that now converge. The agreements are: (1) Christ crucified and risen is "the once-for-all sacrifice for the sins of the world who gives himself to the faithful . . . in the Lord's Supper." (2) "The celebration of the eucharist is the church's sacrifice of praise and self-offering or oblation."[6]

The four past items of divergence are:

1. Although Trent did affirm that the sacrifice of the cross is "unrepeatable," Lutherans were never totally convinced that the Tridentine church actually practiced it. Today no Catholic theologians dispute that claim of unrepeatability.

2. The language so allergenic for Lutherans, of "offering Christ" in the Mass, does not detract "from the full sufficiency of Christ's sacrifice. The members of the body of Christ are united through Christ with God and with one another in such a way that they become participants in his worship, his self-offering, his sacrifice to the Father. Through this union . . . the eucharistic assembly 'offers Christ' by consenting in the power of the Holy Spirit to be offered by him to the Father."[7] There follows a footnote where Luther is cited as saying the same thing:

> . . . not that we offer Christ as a sacrifice, but that Christ offers us"; but he also holds that this involves a sense in which "we offer Christ": "Through *faith* in connection with the sacrament, we offer ourselves, our need, our prayer, praise and thanksgiving in Christ, and thereby we offer Christ. . . . I also offer Christ in that I desire and *believe* that he accepts me and my prayer and praise and presents it to God in his own person.[8]

Note that in place of Luther's "standard" *sola fide* grounding for such "offering of Christ" the consensus statement speaks of "consenting in the power of the Holy Spirit." Is this a signal of moving away from faith as the point at issue? See the "Comment" section below.

3. No longer is "propitiatory" a conflict point since Roman Catholics today say that Christ's cross is the unique propitiatory sacrifice "efficacious for the forgiveness of sins and the life of the world." Lutherans' historic allergy to "sacrifice offered for the living and the dead" was left unattended in these discussions.

4. There is significant convergence in the actual practice of eucharistic worship. E.g., Vatican II pushes practice away from private Masses to congregational celebrations.[9]

On the disputed point of presence there are areas where both partners speak with one voice:[10] (1) Christ's manifold presence in the world; (2) His presence "wholly and entirely" in the Lord's

Supper; (3) The variety of formulations to describe that presence along with a common rejection of Capernaitic realism and a commemorative or figurative manner of presence, coupled with a new appreciation of the term "sign" for speaking of Christ's presence; (4) Christ's presence is not generated by the faith of the believer, nor the power of the celebrant, but by the Holy Spirit through the word; (5) Christ's presence continues throughout the eucharistic action; (6) Communion under both kinds is recognized by Rome as the better practice.

On the transubstantiation issue Roman theology's reworking of it sounds appropriate to the Lutherans. Both partners are persuaded that no single framework or vocabulary can be adequate, exclusive, or final. Their concluding sentence: "We are convinced that current theological trends in both traditions give great promise for increasing convergence and deepened understanding of the eucharistic mystery."[11]

Comment

The faith agenda does not surface in the official statement, and only via the footnote mentioned above, claiming Luther's support for our "offering Christ" in the Lord's Supper, is it mentioned. But its import is not noticed, and that is a bit strange, for the citation comes from one of the essays published in the volume. Ironically, the author is a Roman Catholic lay theologian, James McCue, whose article "Luther and Roman Catholicism on the Mass as Sacrifice"[12] exegetes Luther's *A Treatise on the New Testament* (NT = Lord's Supper) and finds some important quotes about the Mass as sacrifice. But McCue sees how all the prosacrifice statements are grounded by the *sola fide*, with its christological corollary of the Lord's Supper as Christ's New Testament, Jeremiah's "new covenant," the promise of forgiveness.

Though not totally absent from the Lutheran–Roman Catholic dialogues as far as I have tracked them, these terms (faith, promise, testament, and sign) never receive central attention, though they are occasionally mentioned. One might deduce that *sola fide* is a given and thus irrelevant to settling the remaining sacramental sore spots. But that was hardly the case in 1966–67, as witnessed to by how many years it took to produce the convergence statement on justification by faith.

McCue brings the *sola fide* into the sacrifice discussion by introducing an item from Luther that did not make it into the *Book of Concord*. Thus it is not confessionally canonical.

Nevertheless, why did the Lutherans not do something with this gift offered by "the other side"?

Of course, the same material is there in the confessional documents. The Melanchthon citation at the beginning of this essay (the conflict with Rome on Eucharist is a *sola fide* conflict) introduces his own theological construction for eucharistic theology built with the same building blocks that McCue's Luther uses. Twenty-five times in Apology 13 and 24 he uses "New Testament" as his key term for the Eucharist. Not at all is he talking about the twenty-seven canonical books. He is talking about the "new deal" that has come in Christ and that is "offered" in the Lord's Supper. For Melanchthon the Lord's Supper is not Christ's sacrifice at all. The focus is not on the first Good Friday. It is on the first Easter Sunday. Thus Maundy Thursday is proleptically Easter Sunday. The Lord's Supper is the distribution of the benefits of the sacrifice. It is not a revisioning of the Good Friday sacrifice in any significant sense at all.

Here is a fundamental difference with the Roman adversaries. The Lord's Supper for Melanchthon is a consequence of Good Friday, not a return to it. That is why he prefers *sacramentum* as his key term in place of *sacrificium*, even if the sacrifice would be clearly designated as Christ's own. "A sacrament is a ceremony or act in which God offers us the content of the promise [of Christ's sacrifice]" (Ap 24:17; BC 252). Thus sacrament is the consequence of the sacrifice. He claims that this definition is not his own. "The theologians make a proper distinction between sacrament and sacrifice" (Ap 24:17; BC 252).

All of his labor later on to distinguish propitiatory and eucharistic sacrifices is, he feels, pressed upon him by the Roman *Confutatores* who will not allow the discussion to run on the term "sacrament." But if he must use the term sacrifice, he can, of course, do so. And the way he does it is to make New Testament, faith, promise, and sign his rhetoric for "the Mass as sacrifice." If the Lutheran participants did invoke this resource from their own tradition in their discussions, it never got into the published results.

To say that the "real issue" is the *sola fide* is to nuance the controversy of the sixteenth century away from the formal doctrine of the sacrament to the *usus*. For with the Lord's Supper the doing of it has priority over the *teaching* about it. And thus the *usus* question, not primarily the "how do you celebrants do it," but the communicants' *usus*, the "how do you use/receive it," is the "point at issue." That, however, is the *sola fide* question.

Is that not the fundamental ecumenical question in eucharistic matters—the use/uselessness of the Lord's Supper in the lives of Christian people today?

The Dialogue with the Reformed

The Data

Marburg Revisited (1966), in two of its summary statements, rings the changes on the faith factor in the Lord's Supper. Even more faith-"full" were the Arnoldshain Theses of 1957. I cannot track the flow from Arnoldshain to *Marburg Revisited,* but the former must have impacted the latter. The Leuenberg Agreement (1973) also articulates its "common understanding of the gospel" throughout with the fundamental corollary of faith and promise, and its statements about the Lord's Supper are no exception.

Not so the Joint Statement of 1983 from series 3 of the U.S. dialogues. Here the language of Lima, in the *Baptism, Eucharist and Ministry* document, not only supplies new vocabulary, but almost nudges the language of promise/faith off the page, yet stating "we affirm these agreements, in particular . . . *Marburg Revisited* . . . and Leuenberg."[13]

Let us begin with Arnoldshain and note its classical Lutheran vocabulary.

> 4. Our Lord Jesus Christ gives us, as his words promise to those who believe in his promise, the victory of his lordship, forgiveness, and blessedness.

8. Faith receives what is promised to it and builds on this promise
. . . . All members of (the Lord's) church are invited to his meal, and
the forgiveness of sins is promised to all who desire God's righteousness.[14]

Marburg Revisited begins with an affirmation of gospel grounding
as it attempts a "reexamination of our theological formulations in
the light of the word of God." In talking about the Lord's Supper
the text goes on to say, "the sacrament . . . arouses faith through
its presentation of the gospel." Or again, "the presence of Christ
in the sacrament is not effected by faith, but acknowledged by faith.
The worthy participant is the one who receives in faith and repentance
the Christ who offers himself in the sacrament."[15]

Leuenberg confesses a "common understanding of the gospel"
that begins with the message of justification for Christ's sake by
faith alone and then moves to preaching, baptism, and the Lord's
Supper.

15. In the Lord's Supper the risen Christ imparts himself in his
body and blood, given up for all, through his word of promise with
bread and wine. He thereby grants us forgiveness of sins, and sets us
free for a new life of faith.[16]

In view of the past condemnations between the Lutherans and the
Reformed, Leuenberg says: "We take the decisions of the Reformation fathers seriously, but are today able to agree on the following
in respect to these condemnations":

18. In the Lord's Supper the risen Jesus Christ imparts himself in
his body and blood, given up for all, through his word of promise
with bread and wine. He thus gives himself unreservedly to all who
receive the bread and wine; faith receives the Lord's Supper for salvation, unfaith for judgment.
19. We cannot separate communion with Jesus Christ in his body
and blood from the act of eating and drinking. To be concerned about
the manner of Christ's presence in the Lord's Supper in abstraction
from this act is to run the risk of obscuring the meaning of the Lord's
Supper.
20. Where such a consensus exists between the churches, the condemnations pronounced by the Reformation confessions are inappli-
cable to the doctrinal positions of these churches.[17]

The closest that the Joint Statement of 1983 comes to this Lutheran trajectory is in a footnote where Regin Prenter is cited making the case for such sacramental theology.

> In every sacrament there is a divine *promissio* expressed in the Word which accompanies the sacrament. This *promissio* is the decisive factor. It is what makes the sacrament a sacrament. By virtue of understanding the word of the sacrament as *promissio* faith enters into the concept of the sacrament in the sense that it thus forms the real connection between the Word and the external element. For the external element is the confirmation of the promise. But only faith in the promise can receive the confirmation.[18]

The Joint Statement begins its first article (on the gospel) affirming "fidelity to the gospel as the fundamental norm" for all theology. Thus "it is from the gospel that we understand the Lord's Supper. . . . The Supper is itself a particular form of the gospel."[19] When, however, it comes to saying just what this particular form actually is (article 2), a reticence to say anything particular surfaces. Generalities, even truisms, take over in the text. Several times we are told that "all of us need continually to grow" and above all that "the Lord's Supper is inexhaustibly profound and awesome." This much they are able to say: that they "concur" with the Lima statement (BEM) and its fivefold matrix for articulating the "fullness of the Lord's Supper."

The third article of the Joint Statement of 1983 ("The New Community") does make reference to "the community of faith," "the fellowship of believers," who "trust in God's faithfulness."[20] Thus the faith focus is not absent, at least rhetorically. One sentence that still explicitly echoes the Lutheran memory states: "As we participate in the Holy Communion we receive the benefits of the forgiveness of sins, life and salvation through our trust in God's faithfulness." Although that is the first of four benefits arising "as we participate in the Holy Communion," it does not assume any determinative role for the ones that follow. The Lima document's "five-for-fullness" is paralleled in these "four-for-those-fed" at the eucharistic meal.

The last two articles of the Joint Statement (Doctrine, Practice) "affirm that the Lutheran and Reformed families of churches have

a fundamental consensus in the gospel and the sacraments."[21] Therefore "remaining differences should be recognized as acceptable
diversities within one Christian faith."[22]

Comment

The conclusion reached in the Joint Statement of 1983 is the same
as *Marburg Revisited,* The Arnoldshain Theses, and Leuenberg, but
the path to that same conclusion operates with a different compass.
Is it a better way? I think not.

Was it ecumenical etiquette post-Lima that urged this less than
Lutheran *and* less than Reformed avenue? Perhaps. Yet are we not
at the place where ecumenical etiquette no longer requires that the
conversation partners hide it under a bushel? Nowadays the way to
confront pluralism is to confront it and not shilly-shally in devel-
opmental agnosticism. But to confront pluralism head-on is itself
an act of faith, specifically faith in the promise that we will survive
the ordeal, that, as Christ said, even the gates of hell shall not prevail
against us.

I can, of course, not address the "faith factor" or its absence in
the heart of the dialogue participants. And to do so in their absence
is gossip. My assignment is to address what they put down on paper.
My thesis about that is that Melanchthon is correct: the *sola fide* is
the "real issue" in the dialogues about the Lord's Supper.

1. Measured by that thesis the dialogues reviewed are a mixed bag.
The LED never touches it. Even if the Episcopalians would never
have brought it up, why did not the Lutherans? And if they did, what
happened? If they did not, why not?

2. In the Lutheran–Reformed dialogues we have been served the
reverse of the menu at the wedding at Cana. Instead of saving the
best until last, after Marburg, Arnoldshain, and Leuenberg, the last
is the poorer wine.

3. In the eucharistic dialogue with Roman Catholics the *sola fide*
got in by a footnote from James McCue's masterful essay, but did
not play any major role in the joint statement. But in the subsequent
history of this dialogue, it has finally surfaced. It was not merely
ecumenical caution that placed the justification by faith item almost
fifteen years down the road in these dialogues. The dialogue partners

were finally pushed into it by the very topics they addressed beforehand. This dialogue has not skirted the article of *faith alone*, but has finally addressed it head on. Is that a sign for other bilateral dialogues? Neither today's church nor today's world has any more important agenda.

11

Ministry

Daniel F. Martensen

The purpose of these observations is not to solve the difficult theological problems surrounding the ministry issue, but to discuss in a selective fashion where we are right now in facing the issue itself. As a limiting principle, three basic questions are asked of the material: What is the purpose, place, and profile of the ordained ministry in the church? Have Lutherans been consistent in their bilateral conversations when considering ministry? What is the bilateral dialogue challenge to Lutheran ecclesial self-understanding? With these questions as background, in Part One we will deal with the following aspects of ministry as they are reflected in the documentation: ecclesial basis of ordained ministry, apostolic succession and the office of the bishop, and mutual recognition of ministries. In Part Two and in the conclusion remarks will be made about the ecclesiological question which rightfully pervades the entire discussion on ministry.

Resource material used is limited to the world level and the North American regional bilateral results of conversations with the Roman Catholic, Anglican, and Reformed communities, with some reference to the Baptists, Methodists, Conservative/Evangelicals, and Orthodox.[1]

I. Aspects of Ministry

It should be noted from the outset that the authors of the various reports on ministry make no attempt to lay out a thorough and detailed presentation of any specific topic. The reports tend to stress the controversial issues in the context of the basic assumptions of the two communions involved.

A. The Ecclesial Basis of Ordained Ministry

Statements made in the U.S.A. Lutheran–Roman Catholic report on *Eucharist and Ministry* (1970) accent the ministry of the people of God and the special ministry; they serve as one point of reference for the international Malta and Pullach reports. There is no statement in the U.S.A. document which could be considered contradictory to those made at the world level.[2]

The 1972 Roman Catholic–Lutheran Malta Report ties the foundation of ministry to the gospel because the "witness of the gospel requires that there be witnesses to the gospel" (#48). Another line of argumentation points to the emergence of a special ministry in New Testament times which is connected with the apostles and with the charisms which are given to the whole church (##51–54). The Anglican–Lutheran Pullach Report (1972) accents the second line of argumentation which combines the theological and the historical. It says the ministry "was instituted by God through Jesus Christ in the sending of the apostles" (#75).

The world-level Lutheran–Roman Catholic Joint Commission's 1981 statement on *The Ministry in the Church* draws heavily upon the Malta Report but then moves on to accent the pneumatological and christological bases of ministry in order to clarify questions of authority. It affirms that "the christologically based authority (*exousia*) of the ministry must be exercised in the Holy Spirit" (#22). In its basic argumentation the report restates the position on ordination reflected in the U.S.A., Malta, and Pullach reports.

The Pullach Report stresses God's action in ordination through the whole church, the authority given through ordination, prayer, and laying on of hands, and the special ministry (#78). The U.S.A. and Malta reports deal with the sacramental character of ordination. Malta mentions laying on of hands and invoking of the Holy Spirit (#59) and the fact that neither of the churches repeats ordination

(#60). Concerning the sacramental nature of ordination the world-level Lutheran–Catholic document of 1981 cites the traditional differences between the two communions and then says:

> Wherever it is taught that through the act of ordination the Holy Spirit gives grace strengthening the ordained person for the life-time ministry of word and sacrament, it must be asked whether differences which previously divided the churches on this question have not been overcome. (#33)

The Lutheran–Episcopal Dialogue 2 (1976–80) begins where the Pullach Report stopped. On this issue, however, it does not modify the basic position taken in 1972.

Turning to the Reformed–Lutheran conversations, one notes immediately that the Leuenberg Agreement reached by the European churches in 1973 did not address the ministry question. It was the belief of the drafters of Leuenberg that ministry was not among the issues which is church dividing. They did, however, note that in the continuing doctrinal conversations which were to follow Leuenberg ministry and ordination were to be among the main topics discussed.

One of the three major joint statements to emerge from the U.S.A. Lutheran–Reformed Dialogue Series 3 (1981–83) was on ministry. In its affirmation that the traditions in the dialogue are rooted in a common understanding of the gospel which developed in the Reformation, the dialogue team goes on to relate the servant ministry of Jesus to our ministry. This theme runs through the paragraphs on the ministry and the kingdom of God, the ministry and the entire people of God, and the pastoral office.

The statement makes it clear that Lutheran and Reformed Christians agree on the nature and function of the ordained ministry. However, it immediately goes on to point to a problematic area, the ordination of elders and deacons. Both traditions see ministry as an apostolic office centered in the preaching of the word and the administration of the sacraments and anchored in the Confessions and creeds of the church. The Reformed tradition has set the pastoral office in a broader ministerium which includes ordained elders and deacons who share the oversight of the church and ministries of compassion and justice.[3]

In 1979 the Lutheran–United Methodist Dialogue Team adopted a statement on baptism. The only reference made to ministry is:

Each denomination affirms the pastoral and nurturing ministry of the other denomination and gladly commits members to the care of the other denomination when its own denomination does not provide an adequate congregational family for those members.[4]

Then in 1987 the Lutheran–Methodist Dialogue completed a study of episcopacy in which they concluded "we acknowledge God's gift of an ordained ministry, the public pastoral office. . . . Lutherans and Methodists alike affirm this ministry as necessary to the church."[5]

In 1981 the Lutheran–Baptist conversations in the U.S.A. developed a common statement on church and ministry and, despite divergences, found profound bases for commonality. Both communions claimed to be evangelical; both saw the church to be the "fellowship of the people of God, the body of the living Christ"; both affirmed the church as "the company of those who have been justified by God's grace, regenerated by the Holy Spirit, and incorporated by baptism into a visible community of faith." Concerning ordination they said: ". . . we believe there is a special office of the ordained ministry which has a divine calling and a particular function within the common ministry of the whole body of believers."[6]

In 1981 the Lutheran–Conservative/Evangelical dialogue stated in its declaration:

We acknowledge that our Lord has called us into his body, the Church. The Church lives by his gifts of grace. We acknowledge the importance of baptism, the Lord's Supper, and the exercise of spiritual discipline in the Church, without having attained a consensus concerning the definition of those ministries and offices.[7]

In the individual reports there appear to be no statements which are contradictory on the ecclesial bases for ordained ministry. The reports do not offer a complete description of ordination; one may mention elements lacking in the other. The fuller exposition in the U.S.A. *Eucharist and Ministry* is not contradicted by what is written later in the Malta and Pullach reports, for example. The statements are complementary.

B. Apostolic Succession and the Office of the Bishop

In these paragraphs as in the ones preceding, the U.S.A. *Eucharist and Ministry* text and the Malta and Pullach reports from the early 1970s are foundational. The U.S.A. text asserts that the ministry is apostolic. "The term 'apostolic' has had a variety of references: it has been applied, for instance, to doctrine, practices, authority."[8]

The Malta and the Pullach reports affirm a similar starting point. Apostolic succession is expressed primarily through the apostolicity of the entire church which is faithful to the apostolic witness. The Malta Report argues from historical grounds (#57 and #58), while the comprehensive character of the apostolic succession of the whole church and the multiple means of its expression and preservation through time is accented in the Pullach Report (##73–75). Catholics see this special ministerial succession as a sign of the unimpaired transmission of the gospel and as a sign of unity in the faith. Lutherans grant the importance of this as long as succession in the gospel remains preeminent and succession in ministry does not become a guarantee of the right proclamation of the gospel (#57).

Ministry of word and sacrament, of pastoral care and oversight, is seen in the Anglican–Lutheran Pullach Report as one of the several ways the "succession of apostolicity through time is guarded and given contemporary expression" (#74). The report then affirms that all who have been called and ordained to the ministry in obedience to the apostolic faith "stand together in the succession of office" (#77).

The Lutheran–Episcopal Dialogue 2 (1980, U.S.A.) underlines the fact that both communions recognize the necessity of oversight (*episcopé*) which is embodied in an ordained office. "Lutherans see *episcopé* exercised in the ministry of parish pastors as well as in bishops' supervision of local congregations and clergy, while Episcopalians see that *episcopé* as shared by bishops with their clergy."[9] In spite of the fact that there is serious divergence in the ordering of the pastoral office between the two communions as well as in the significance accorded to the historic episcopate, the dialogue commission said: "We can declare together that both the Lutheran Church and the Episcopal Church stand in Apostolic Succession."[10]

The Roman Catholic–Lutheran Joint Commission at the world level gave special attention to the episcopate in its document on the ministry (1981). Some new ground was broken when the report addressed the relationship between bishop and pastor. The commission agreed that "the existence of local congregational ministries and superordinated regional ministries on both sides is for both churches more than a result of purely historical and human developments or a matter of sociological necessity." They see in this the action of the Spirit; ministry is seen both "in and over against" the ecclesial community. If both churches acknowledge that this development of the one apostolic ministry into a more local and regional ministry constitutes something essential for the church, then the commission affirms, "a *high degree of agreement* has been reached" (#49; italics in the text).

For Catholics the *communio* between the local churches and their bishop is the point of reference for communion with the Church of Rome and the bishop of Rome. The dialogue was led quite naturally to a consideration of the question of universal ministry. No conclusions were reached, but the commission could say in various dialogues, "the *possibility* begins to emerge that the Petrine office of the Bishop of Rome also need not be excluded by Lutherans as a visible sign of unity of the church as a whole, insofar as [this office] is subordinated to the primacy of the gospel by theological reinterpretation and practical restructuring" (Malta par. 66).[11]

In its report on ministry and oversight the LuthDialogue 3 (U.S.A.) underlines the fact that both traditions agree that oversight is necessary. Even though the title "bishop" is rarely used in Reformed churches while it is common among Lutherans, the dialogue team notes that Lutheran polity, like the Reformed, is constitutional. All functions of Lutheran bishops in North America are carried out in relationship to a synod, district, or church body. Because "both ecclesial families claim to stand in the historical and apostolic tradition," and because both traditions "assert that proper oversight is requisite to ensure that the word is truly preached and sacraments rightly administered," the team concludes: "We agree that there are no substantive matters concerning ministry which should divide us.

We urge Lutheran and Reformed churches to affirm and recognize the validity of one another's ministries."[12]

In 1987 the Lutheran–United Methodist Dialogue on episcopacy made mission the "most important standard by which all ministries within the Church are to be judged."[13] "The constant application of this criterion is part of the necessary oversight (*episcopé*) of ministry that must occur within the Church."[14] "We do not, however, understand this oversight to be the exclusive prerogative of the bishop. . . . The episcopal office is not of the essence of Church." "United Methodists and Lutherans understand the distinctive ministry of the bishop to be a form of the single ordained ministry."[15] "An understanding in which other ministries become intrinsically subordinate to, under the control of, or derived from the ministry of the bishop is to be rejected."[16]

Further, "As their ministry of oversight focuses on the pure preaching and teaching of the gospel, bishops serve the unity of the Church. . . . Neither Lutherans nor United Methodists equate the visible unity of the Church with the unity of the episcopate. Nevertheless, we are open to discussion of the special ecumenical role that may be played by bishops and the episcopacy."[17]

C. Mutual Recognition

". . . we recommend to those who have appointed us that through appropriate channels the participating Lutheran churches be urged to declare formally their judgment that the ordained ministers of the Roman Catholic church are engaged in a valid ministry of the gospel. . . ."[18]

". . . we ask the authorities of the Roman Catholic church whether the ecumenical urgency flowing from Christ's will for unity may not dictate that the Roman Catholic church recognize the validity of the Lutheran Ministry. . . ."[19]

These rather formidable recommendations were written in 1970 by the respective teams of the Lutheran–Roman Catholic dialogue in the U.S.A. Their counterparts in the world-level dialogue commission argue more cautiously. The Catholic participants ask their authorities to look at the question of the recognition of Lutheran ministries. They ground this request in the recognition by Vatican

II of the ecclesial character of the non-Roman Catholic churches. They point to the emergency situation of the Reformation period (as does the U.S.A. group) and to considerations of the charismatic origin of ministries and of the possibility of presbyterial succession (#76). Lutherans, on the other hand, say they do not deny the existence of the office of the ministry in the Roman Catholic Church. They base this on the central Lutheran criteria: true proclamation of the gospel and right administration of the sacraments. Nevertheless, they say it is appropriate for the Lutheran church to examine the question of an explicit recognition of the Roman Catholic ministerial office (##79–80).

The matter was dealt with further by the world-level Lutheran–Roman Catholic Joint Commission in its 1981 report on ministry. In exploring future possibilities of mutual recognition of ministries, it asserts that mutual recognition must not be seen as an isolated act or carried out as such. "It must occur in the confession of the one faith in the context of the unity of the church and in the celebration of the Lord's Supper, the sacrament of unity" (#82). To their mind "the only theologically meaningful way of solving this question is through a process in which the churches reciprocally accept each other" (#82).

It is the conviction of the Joint Commission that mutual recognition can come about only gradually. The stages lead from a mutual respect of ministries through practical cooperation to full recognition, which is identical to the acceptance of eucharistic fellowship. A concrete step to be taken now, they say, is to engage in a process of reception of the findings of previous ecumenical dialogues on ministry (#84).

The Anglican–Lutheran conversations have followed a similar path. In the Pullach Report the Anglican delegates justify the recognition of Lutheran ministries as truly apostolic because "they see in the Lutheran Communion true proclamation of the word and celebration of the Sacraments." As a consequence they "gladly recognize in the Lutheran Church a true communion of Christ's Body, possessing a truly apostolic ministry" (#85). The Anglican representatives draw two further consequences: (1) Recognition, if reciprocal, would permit some form of intercommunion (#86); (2)

Integration of ministries would not be possible apart from the historic episcopate (#87).

Comparably, the ecclesiological criterion is basic to the Lutheran argument for recognition of Anglican ministries. Lutherans see in the Anglican communion true proclamation of the gospel and right administration of the sacraments. These churches are "true apostolic churches and their ministry 'is' an apostolic ministry in unbroken succession" (#90). It follows then that the Lutherans point to intercommunion, exchange of ministers, or full church union (#91) as next steps.

In summary it must be said that a basically consistent Lutheran position emerges in the different reports. There are, however, differences in approach and selection of aspects and emphases in the issues discussed. Each dialogue partner is unique; so too is the shape of the dialogue.

Basic Reformation convictions inform the Lutheran position taken in the conversations. Nevertheless, as the more recent dialogue reports suggest, new seas are now being explored. Theological considerations about *episcopé* and the episcopate, the priestly character of ministry, and apostolic succession have not occupied a prominent place in the Lutheran theological tradition. It is precisely these kinds of issues which have come up in the most advanced dialogues and have raised basic ecclesiological questions. To a few of these we now turn our attention.

II. The Ecclesiology Question

Churches around the world, including many of our sister Lutheran churches, are presently attempting to make official responses to the results of dialogue. The most basic ecclesiological issue emerging from this process is not whether there is Lutheran theological consistency on issues discussed; it is rather the issue of ecclesiology as it relates to the goal of dialogue. What kind of unity do we Lutherans manifest? Toward what kind of Christian unity are we moving? Where is closer fellowship leading? Answers to these questions abound in present ecumenical discourse: "conciliar fellowship," "reconciled diversity," "full visible unity," "organic unity," "restoration of communion of faith and sacramental life," "full mutual recognition of church and ministry," "a communion of communions." The list could continue. One example may help to clarify the issue.

"Full communion between our two churches" has been set as the aim of Lutheran–Anglican relations at the world level. As stated earlier, a claim is made in that global-level conversation that there are no longer any serious obstacles on the way towards the establishment of full communion between the two churches. But what is meant by full communion? Is it synonymous with organic union? What implications does it have for structural expression at the global, regional, and local levels? A statement made in the report of the Joint Working Group suggests that the two churches become interdependent while remaining autonomous. This suggestion begs the question of the conciliar idea as it relates to that of reconciled diversity and as it finds structural expression in a common ministry.

Simply put, the dialogues on the ministry have raised the basic question about a vision of unity. It may be that significant progress on the unresolved theological and ecclesiastical problems of *episcopé* and episcopate, the priestly character of ministry, and apostolic succession will be possible only in the context of a growing consensus on an ecclesiological vision.

In a paper recently prepared for the international level Anglican–Roman Catholic dialogue Mary Tanner suggests some basic ingredients of an ecclesiological vision. They include (1) a deepening of the concept of *koinonia* as participation in the divine trinitarian life (a fundamental in Orthodox Christian life); (2) an emphasis on the eschatological reality already present in human history; (3) an acknowledgment of the relationship of the church to the world; (4) a recognition that any unity which bypasses diversity is a pale reflection of what unity ought to be; and, (5) some clarification of the model of unity, particularly of those structures which will serve and facilitate unity.[20]

We Lutherans have moved in a significant and somewhat dramatic direction in recent years in relationship to the first and last ingredients of the ecclesiological vision just described by Mary Tanner. First, there is a growing awareness of the universality of the church (in space and time) among us. This increased consciousness of the church's universality is certainly directly related to the spiritual discoveries of the unity and catholicity of the church made possible by the modern ecumenical movement which began in the 1920s. Increasing Lutheran affirmation of the episcopal office and structure is a direct result of this deepening awareness of the church's universality. The results of the post-Leuenberg doctrinal discussions in Europe as well as the Lutheran World Federation's consultation on the episcopal office underline this worldwide trend. In the two instances just cited, incidentally, there was no pressure exerted by the Anglican, Roman Catholic, or Orthodox communions upon Lutherans to urge them to move in that direction. This leads to a concluding comment.

Conclusion

It is apparent that bilateral dialogue in conjunction with multilateral conversation has led Lutherans to a crucial juncture in our history. We have come face to face with the fact that ecumenical encounter cannot take place without each church in the dialogue reviewing and modifying its own inherited, traditional position on the question of ministry. In fact that has happened. The result is that the wider Lutheran community, indeed the Lutheran world communion, is being challenged to implement in its life the ecumenical advances which have been made. A summary of one aspect of this advance put in propositional form reads something like the following:

1. The Reformers intended to safeguard the sovereignity of the gospel in and over the church by including ecclesial ministry as closely as possible in word and sacrament, not by excluding it from the definition of the church.

2. The modern ecumenical movement has had the salutary effect upon us Lutherans of leading us away from the individualism-oriented, Enlightenment-rooted idea that the office of the ministry is exclusively a functional one, an office which merely engages in the *activity* of preaching the word and administering the sacrament. We have come to see that the ordained ministry is implied in the jproclamation of the gospel by word and sacrament, as our minimalist confessional ecclesiological definition affirms.

3. Recent dialogue has moved us beyond the often-stated goal of mutual recognition of ministries to a new insight into the need for an episcopal ordering of the church and for *episcopé*. Episcopal ordering is seen to be one of the means affirmed to safeguard and further the unity and catholicity of the church. This affirmation recognizes that church unity requires more than a coexistence of different ministries and certainly does not imply that Lutherans adopt the *episcopé* as it presently exists in some Lutheran churches, the Roman Catholic Church, or the Anglican communion.

4. The challenge of establishing a common ministry requires that ministries enter into communion with each other, a possibility which in one instance urges Lutherans to enter into communion with the historic episcopate.

In selecting this specific focus of bilateral activity we do not mean to suggest that all bilateral advance converges in the Lutheran–Roman Catholic International Joint Commission's document, *Facing Unity*.[21] It is, however, in *Facing Unity* that the basic ecclesiological issue of ministry is posed most pointedly. What we suggest is the following:

If we Lutherans are interested in receiving the results of theological dialogue, we can find no better place to begin than officially and comprehensively to address the proposals laid out in *Facing Unity*. This task must be carried out in light of all other bilateral results and the WCC's convergence statement, *Baptism, Eucharist and Ministry*. These proposals encourage us to move from careful reflection on the early church to the implementation of a process leading to the exercise of a ministry of fellowship. This process is to include engaging in a joint exercise of *episcopé* involving an initial act of recognition, collegial exercise of *episcopé*, and a gradual transition to common ordained ministry.

Postscript

Decades of dialogue are now behind us. Lutherans most intensively involved in it will admit that dialogue done in good faith leads to an ecumenizing of the Lutheran memory. That is, we have learned to incorporate into our life and thought pasts which we have not lived. We have learned how unproductive it is to convert private or denominational theological perspectives into ecclesiological or ecumenical determinants. The ecumenical movement has quite rightly taught us Lutherans that engaging in dialogue is not comparable to the activity of lonely sentinels entering the battle of their private wars waiting for the masses to be sufficiently roused to raise their banners openly. We have learned that the ecumenical movement is inseparable from the quest for the internal renewal of our churches and moving toward our common center, Jesus Christ.

12

Eucharist and Ministry

John Reumann

We are to reflect in this essay on the ministry "across the board" in recent discussions. As a presentation it is able happily to draw on specifics in the survey by Daniel F. Martensen, "Ministry," but it also takes into consideration multilateral discussions, particularly the Faith and Order "Lima text," *Baptism, Eucharist and Ministry*[1] (usually cited below from the Ministry section as "M" plus the paragraph number). I have followed here something of the organizational approach found in my book, *The Supper of the Lord*,[2] which deals with the Eucharist in both bilateral dialogues and in BEM, allowing for the differences in the topics.

1. Few matters are more church-divisive than how leadership is to be organized for ministering. This has been true for a long time, not simply since the Reformation. For already in the New Testament period the evidence is quite varied. J. D. G. Dunn, for example, finds it the least tractable area of all topics in early Christian faith and life in his *Unity and Diversity in the New Testament*. He compares the way lines of thought and praxis in the first century emerge, disappear, combine, and appear as new tracks in the second century with the strands of roadway at the worst of British traffic interchanges, a "spaghetti-junction," no neat cloverleaf, no single superhighway or three-level system, just confusing, yet rich variety.[3]

2. We do well to remember that in recent ecumenical discussion "ministry" has usually been taken up in a certain isolation as a

topic; indeed, often just facets of it appear as the issue under discussion: the ordination of women, the place of bishops, the role of laity, and the like. There is need for a totality of approach. Yet what shall be the context?

3. Lutherans, with their penchant for moving from the gospel or word of God to any particular topic, do well to remember that a biblical, theological, gospel, "word of God" setting is more often assumed than openly stated in many of the dialogue treatments on the ministry. Thus, e.g., for Lima one ought to keep in mind what the Faith and Order meeting in 1963 at Montreal had said about such matters as Scripture and tradition as a background for BEM.[4] Since bilaterals deal with topics that are church-dividing in themselves, such a "background" may never be overtly referred to in their statements. A splendid exception is the statement from series 1 in the international Lutheran–Roman Catholic dialogue. On this score the L–RC Malta Report of 1972, "The Gospel and the Church," is a model for treating the topic on Lutheran grounds.[5] Of course, such a background may be in the minds of participants without articulating it in statements, but the gospel setting is not always put into writing.

A. The Biblical Norms

4. BEM may be taken as an excellent starting point on at least two scores, each of which thoroughly reflects what a great deal of recent New Testament study has had to say in the area of ministry.

a. The BEM discussion begins with "The Calling of *the Whole People of God*" (M §§1–6; italics added). This seems no mere lip service but an understanding that has left its mark on almost every church; compare even and especially the documents of Vatican II. It is the thought of Ephesians 4:11–13 writ large, Ephesians 4:12 correctly punctuated, as in more recent editions of the RSV: the four types of leaders (apostles, prophets, evangelists, pastor-teachers) equip the people of God who *themselves* do "the work of ministry" and build up the body of Christ, for unity of faith.

b. As for "forms of [what becomes] the *ordained ministry*," M §19 serves admirably; there is no "single pattern" but "a variety of forms." It is only in the second and third centuries, BEM emphasizes, that a "threefold pattern of bishop, presbyter and deacon became established." (The later date is more realistic.)

5. We may spell out briefly here some further observations on the New Testament evidence[6] in the following points.

a. The background for Christian ministries does *not* lie in Old Testament models of temple and priesthood. Invoking of such precedents comes only later and outside the canonical writings, though elements of such an approach appear as early as 1 Clement in A.D. 96, where they are mentioned as part of an illustration of order in the world, a virtue prized at Rome.

b. Quite apart from the fact that we know little about the organization of the movement around Jesus (save that it has a treasurer!), we cannot appeal to the historical period of his ministry for structuring Christian ministry. What should be readily apparent here is that we cannot think of "the officers of the ecclesia" assembled in the Upper Room on the final night of Jesus' earthly life as a directing model for the later church through their linear successors, as nineteenth century divines still sometimes put it, any more than we can move directly from what Jesus literally said over bread and wine (as recoverable in Aramaic from our conflicting gospel *verba*) to a doctrine of the Lord's Supper in later centuries. The influence from Jesus was to be christological—in serving.[7]

c. The earliest church was probably more fluid, more charismatic, and more oriented to living within and carrying over some synagogue practices than many Lutherans might be comfortable with. There was thus bold freedom in the Spirit and a respect for the democracy of the synagogue as the "house of study" of the local community and its structures.[8]

d. Our chief evidence on ministries in the New Testament comes from the letters of Paul and the writings of Luke-Acts (among Luke's works I do *not* reckon there to be a third volume, what we call the Pastoral Epistles, as some now claim). But one must be careful not to mix the two, to "lucanize" Paul any more than we should "paulinize" Matthew or John. I find myself most impressed in Paul with his concept of an apostolic authority that is intertwined with that of the "truth of the gospel" (Gal. 2:5, 14) and with his apparent adaptation of varied local forms of leadership for the house churches he planted. Colossians-Ephesians and the Pastorals represent further developments in the Pauline sphere. While Luke appears to be a writer who focuses his thought on Jerusalem as the center out of which true Christianity comes, and was thus an early "centralist," it should be remembered that his very mixed picture is the court of appeal also for charismatics and pneumatics, as well as for those favoring hierarchy and organization from "headquarters." But one does not find historically combined in the New Testament, even in the Pastoral Epistles, Lucan "elders" (presbyters) together with Pauline *episkopoi kai diakonoi* (Phil. 1:1, "overseers who also serve"?).[9]

e. Along with this tendency to find organizational lines to later centuries in Luke and Paul, one must bear in mind the extremely varied and different sorts of leadership and polity in the Matthean community (23:34, a college of prophets, the wise, and scribes?); in 1 Peter; and in the Johannine community, to take just three examples.[10] First Peter 2:9-10 is, of course, the basis for later appeals both about "priesthood" and a "priesthood of all believers." J. Elliott's study, *The Elect and the Holy* (1966),[11] is widely cited in New Testament circles and in dialogues on this passage for its demonstration that a corporate group is intended who show forth God's "wonderful deeds" in missionary service. But one must be aware that Elliott has changed his mind on certain details in his more recent study, *A Home for the Homeless* (1981); here he holds that we deal sociologically with an alienated group for whom their new *oikos pneumatikos* (2:5) is not a "spiritual temple" but a "house [community] in which the Spirit dwells."[12] As for Johannine community, "the community of the beloved disciple," if Raymond E. Brown is even partially correct in his analysis, we have here a band of sisters and brothers with little organization, as far as ministry goes, but a high Christology as their faith identification for life.[13]

6. The old account (the German was originally published in 1959) by Eduard Schweizer, *Church Order in the New Testament,* is still a helpful and basically correct orientation to the varieties of ministry in the New Testament. Subsequent studies have carried that variety further in its scope and detail. Dunn's chapter, mentioned in paragraph (1) above, is a good updating, and an impressive array of

literature continues to appear.[14] Among Catholics Edward Schille-beeckx (most recently, *The Church with a Human Face*, 1985) is but one of many writers who reflects and works from these studies, carries them further, and makes suggestions for Catholic views of the ministry.[15]

7. Probably few of us have paid enough attention to the case set forth on the roles of women in the New Testament church such as Elisabeth Schüssler Fiorenza has provided, notably in her book *In Memory of Her*.[16] While one must be careful not to overdo the evidence, there was quite likely a "patriarchal repression" that set in later on of earlier currents found, e.g., in Jesus, Paul, and the Fourth Gospel.

8. One must also welcome case studies on ministerial leadership in specific geographical regions among Christians, showing at the least the variety of ways in which church structures developed. A good example is Raymond E. Brown and John P. Meier, *Antioch & Rome* (1983).[17] These two cities differed greatly in the types of "catholic Christianity" that developed and in how this came about. What, for example, reversed the Matthean form of governance in Antioch into the Ignatian model in a decade or so, as sketched by this volume, is amazing, if true. I find myself wondering whether each city was so uniform in each case to begin with as the book assumes. May not house churches have varied almost the way later "denominations" do?

9. Can we still speak of biblical *norms* here, when the New Testament turns out to be so pluralistic? Yes, for I think that the New Testament, though with great latitude, does indeed regularly call for ministerial leadership, granted due allowances for situations and backgrounds to make it effective. And it is understood as leadership in ministry that edifies the community (*oikodomē*) for its witnessing tasks, the ministering of the entire group. Perhaps the ecumenical challenge today is to protect the pluralism to which the New Testament pointed.

B. Historical Developments

10. While we cannot trace here all the intricate steps in the eventual development of what BEM terms the "threefold ministry"—which

BEM asks churches to accept, not as demanded by the New Testament but as a development which some churches insist upon as the norm—we can note the cruciality of *Ignatius of Antioch* for the rise of a hierarchial ministry of leadership. It can be agreed that monepiskopos, presbyters, and deacons appear here together for the first time, indeed emphatically. J. Meier is probably correct in saying this structure arose in Ignatius' church to hold the gospel firmly against false teachers (Jews and Gnostics) and in the face of persecution, and he is also right in pointing out that Ignatius himself was "a man of the Spirit."[18] But how shall we assess Ignatius and these developments? There are several possibilities:

Was Ignatius forcefully reshaping the Matthean church structures to meet these new demands? (so Meier)

Was he thus, *iure divino,* providentially providing the pattern God intended for the church thereafter? (This is a traditional view.)

Was he really a successor to Paul (via the Pastorals) and to John?[19]

Was he really not representative of general trends but rather an innovator, representing a new minority view?[20]

Was he a muddle-headed egotist, with a martyr complex? The most recent treatment on Ignatius, by William R. Schoedel, scarcely resolves matters to the satisfaction of all. Schoedel sees in Ignatius episcopacy without succession; there is still a collegial ministry, and overall a Pauline view that is "but a step" beyond the Pastorals; further, Schoedel holds that for Ignatius the leaders were not, as many claim, "divinized." One must go to later fathers for the full development of what becomes threefold ministry.[21]

11. A number of factors played a role in development of "clergy" as over against "laity," in this process. Some of these factors are noted in Bernard Cooke, *Ministry to Word and Sacrament.*[22] These include the *cursus honorum* in the Roman Empire (*ordinatio* comes from *ordinare,* "to put in order"); the hierarchies of Neoplatonism, as mediated through [Pseudo]-Dionysius; the historical situations addressed and a "blessed rage for order"; and an intertwining with certain aspects of ministry, notably celebration of the Eucharist (the need for others than the bishop to preside, hence presbyters; the concept of sacrifice to befit the role of priests, for example).[23]

12. Without tracing out, or trying to trace out, the intricacies of all these developments, such as whether bishops arose from "below" in the presbyterate or were "from above" (and the matter is probably more complicated than these two alternatives), we note that each of the offices in threefold ministry underwent considerable modification in the patristic centuries and Middle Ages.

a. In a real sense it was not always threefold ministry. Sometimes it was as high as sevenfold.

b. The deacon, perhaps originally attached to the bishop as assistant, became attached to the presbyter.

c. The office of bishop expanded in importance. This was due in part to the excellent leadership, including leadership in matters theological, given by some incumbent bishops (Cooke).

d. Eventually the office of deacon shriveled away, at least in the West, becoming a stepping-stone to the priesthood. We can speak not of "threefold ministry" but of "2.3-fold" ministry or something of the sort in many cases.

e. For Rome, though this happened with the diaconate, a new upper echelon emerged in the papacy. Was threefold now pope, bishop, and priest, or was it fourfold (or 3.2)? Sufficient attention has not always been paid to *which* threefold ministry one wishes to insist upon for restoring Christendom.

It is a safe guess that in modern ecumenics it was the Anglicans through their Lambeth Quadrilateral of 1888 who introduced the "Historic Episcopate" as a *sine qua non* into the discussions.[24] Roman Catholics and the Orthodox have, as they have become involved in the ecumenical movement, of course, strengthened this emphasis, but their views are by no means in full agreement with each other. If "threefold ministry" were the solution, why not greater agreement, cooperation, and recognition among these "catholic" traditions? Among them, too, ministry remains at issue.

13. Regarding Lutherans in the Reformation period, one might venture the opinion that for all the debates among the historians the Lutheran insistence was that there must be an ordained ministry, of and over against the community, an ordained ministry to which God and the community (not the individual) call; there is *one office* in this ministry, that of pastor-bishop, and this singular office is entered

through ordination, which might even be called a sacrament if "interpreted in relation to the ministry of the Word" (Ap 13.10; BC 212). That last phrase introduces what must surely be the major new approach in the Lutheran Confessions: the ministry (office of, the ministry of teaching) has been instituted by God in order that we may obtain the faith described in Article 4 of the CA on justification. Ministry is seen in light of justification, ministers as the agents to "move" it to people, and such proclamation (where "the gospel is taught purely and the sacraments are administered rightly") creates the church. CA 3–7 is therefore unusual in the prominence it gives the ministry, ahead of church, in light of gospel. Is this a reflection, we may ask, of Romans 10:14–17?[25]

14. Nonetheless, it must be acknowledged that there are problems even among Lutherans in how to read the Confessions. These problems have to do with which documents determine which, interpretatively, and even within the CA which article(s) is/are the center for interpreting the rest. E.g., on ministry, should CA 28 be the starting point (on the grounds that it was drafted earlier, originally for the Torgau Articles), and therefore one *assumes* bishops, even when reading 3–7 (so Maurer *et al*)?[26] This seems to me to use historical "source analysis," but only to a point, for it then insists on "freezing" the interpretive center at one historical moment in 1530, without asking about subsequent historical developments in the trajectory. Or should one read the document "as its stands," in its redacted form, the CA in the sequence in which it was presented? Or are the subsequent debates and interpretations determinative?[27]

15. On subsequent Lutheran history concerning the doctrine of the ministry, I may refer to my essay, "Ordained Minister and Layman [*sic*] in Lutheranism," written for the U.S. Lutheran–Catholic dialogue in the late 1960s.[28] Of course, much more has been written since then. I find helpful, for illustrating the diversity of European backgrounds that Lutherans brought to the U.S.A. in groups that made up the ALC, the book *Church Roots* and am impressed with the consistency with which Lutherans, even of the most congregational outlook, sought ordination for their ministerial leaders from other Lutheran ministers. Often these other Lutheran ministers whom quite pietistic Lutherans turned to were of rather

"high church" persuasion on the ministry, e.g., the Dane Claus Clausen was ordained by a Buffalo Synod German, L. F. E. Krause.[29]

16. The recent volume by James H. Pragman, *Traditions of Ministry*,[30] is exactly on our subject. The book seems to me to overemphasize Luther on the universal priesthood at the expense of the Confessions on the ordained ministry. (Or is this another hermeneutical question, on the relation of Luther to the Confessions?) Pragman's volume unfortunately stops short of covering the period in which the latest LCMS statement on "The Ministry" (1981) has appeared.

17. In light of discussions within the Commission for a New Lutheran Church (1982–86) concerning Christian day school teachers, I would now have to rewrite the passing observations in my 1970 paper for the Catholic dialogue on that topic. The AELC and LCMS positions have similarities but are by no means the same, especially regarding women in such roles.[31]

C. Ecumenical Discussions

18. A useful outline for analyzing the host of subissues involved in discussions on the ministry today is provided by Ehrenström and Gassmann, in *Confessions in Dialogue*.[32] These are listed below, with comments, taking into consideration BEM as well as what the Martensen essay has reported on the bilaterals.

a. The relation of ordained to general ministry. As indicated in connection with BEM above, most recent statements begin with at least a nod to the "general" ministry, that of all believers. The U.S. Lutheran–Catholic dialogue, volume 4, provides a good example. Setting the ordained ministry (with all its problems) within the entire ministering people of God not only provides a more biblical context and forces all to new ways of thinking, but also recognizes where laity already are in many cases. The opinion of Pragman is scarcely correct when it is claimed that the importance of the laity and of universal priesthood "has not been a topic of major interest for most twentieth century Lutheran theologians";[33] it certainly has been, especially with many of the laity. To locate ordained ministry within general ministry also allows for attention to the Spirit and to charismata, grace-gifts, as originating factors in ministry (BEM, M §§32–33), not simply institutional structures. Yet there has been a long inner-Lutheran debate in this area; Pragman's book illustrates one side of the issue, favoring general ministry as the source for ordained ministry. Lutherans generally (including I think today much of the Missouri Synod) no longer derive the ordained ministry from the total community by a "transference" of rights to the clergy, who are creations (in this view) of the laity "on sufferance."

b. Apostolicity in Ministry. The question of "succession" to the apostles can be separated from threefold ministry and all "pipeline" views. I regard this question of succession to have been pretty well settled in the dialogues along the lines already indicated by Edmund Schlink in his 1963 address at Montreal, "Apostolic Succession,"[34] namely that there are several types of succession to what the apostles stood for; one can have succession to the apostles' *doctrine* and not simply to their sequential office. Compare the Malta Report (#57) and U. S. Lutheran–Catholic dialogue as illustrations of how this point has been accepted and applied.[35]

c. Episcopacy and Threefold Ministry.[36] The office of the bishop has often emerged as the real point at issue, though Martensen suggests that a trend among Lutherans toward the "affirmation of the episcopal office and structure" reflects "increased consciousness of the church's universality."[37] But what is a "real bishop"? One with more than local connections? One who will not ordain women? Has the issue been solved or plastered over in dialogues by use of the Greek term *episkopé?* Note the frequent use of "fullness" in connection with this ministry. To what extent is this a helpful term?[38]

d. Papal Ministry. BEM ducks this problem area, yet there can be no accord with Rome without a solution. The U.S. Lutheran–Catholic dialogue, series 5, especially dealt with it.[39] ARCIC I hoped it might "be possible to envisage a papal primacy of honour and service, but such a primacy can ultimately be justified only as a useful historical development within the life of the Church," i.e., as *iure humano. The Final Report* in 1981 is more complex on *ius divinum* but does view primacy as service and "focus of visible unity in truth and love."[40]

e. Ordination.   Several dialogues have dealt with the topic, generally feeling that traditional differences have been overcome. But does the problem of "how" one is ordained and with what meaning lurk behind the question of mutual recognition?[41]

f. Women.   In BEM, M §18 notes the issue but can really only ask for forbearance. The response of the LCA to BEM on this issue, as in the ALC, was strongly in defense of its experience with women pastors. In the dialogues the international Lutheran–Roman Catholic volume on *The Ministry* (1981) deals with the issue only in its Supplement 1, interestingly written by the bishop of a Lutheran country that at that time had refused to ordain women. But if the ordaining of women is an ecumenical issue, it also remains a point of difference among U.S. Lutherans. It should be remembered that the LCUSA study on the ordination of women concluded that neither Scripture nor doctrine forbids this practice or demands it and that Lutherans throughout the world need not at a given time all hold the same view.[42]

g. Mutual recognition.   Martensen emphasizes that real vision leads beyond this.[43] Was the U.S. Lutheran–Catholic dialogue *avant garde* in 1970? LED 2 has led, however, in this direction via eucharistic sharing.

h. Intercommunion.   Is this the goal or, as now for many, also a step along the way? Many "degrees" of intercommunion are possible.[44] Has it been interpreted too exclusively in "altar" terms rather than in "pulpit" terms as well and in terms of other aspects of fellowship?

D. Questions for Lutherans

19. While one may (or may not) wish to agree that Lutherans have been reasonably consistent in their dialogues with other churches on ministry issues, nonetheless issues remain that concern inner-Lutheran discussions as well as a Lutheran stance toward future dialogues.

a. The BEM proposal grows out of the bilateral dialogues but also confronts each and every dialogue. In my own judgment it is unlikely that a widespread consensus will emerge on the BEM proposal of having all adopt a threefold ministry yet with the understanding that it arose after the New Testament, i.e., that it is *iure humano* but not scripturally *divino*. It is as a proposal both too much and too little. It will prove too much for churches without "episcopal succession" (for what is accepted on pragmatic grounds has a way of making itself seem necessary dogmatically, if not historically); it will prove too little for churches treasuring the historic episcopate and apostolic succession (since they regard these as the *esse* and not merely a luxury and helpful addition). A further question is whether the very terms we have been using, *iure divino/humano*, are still useful. Are most things in the church "of human development" but then taken to be "of the divine will" in retrospect? How can one decide that something is one or the other and not "both/and"?

b. How shall our Lutheran confessional heritage be read, within the CA, within the *Book of Concord*, in relation to Luther, in the face of subsequent events, and in light of the biblical data as now understood?

c. How does the theme of justification relate to ministry? Is it a matter of Protestant message *and* Catholic structure? Shall it be understood in the manner of CA 3–7 as proposed above? Or along lines of Maurer's interpretation? Or have Lutherans in fact given up relating them? Is the experience of justification, as indeed some have suggested is so for the whole New Testament, perpetually directed against our human attempts to build institutional security?

d. Is the Lutheran contribution to the ecumenical world to insist that a doctrine of the ministry is not *iure divino* or simply *iure humano* but *sub specie evangelii*, arising out of the gospel and the need to proclaim it?

e. Do not Lutherans have remarkably little they must defend here? Ministry, which means service (*diakonia*), must involve a *Predigtamt, ministerium docendi evangelii et porrigendi sacramenta*, God-given, with the function of setting forth the gospel of justification. It is a view that has often elevated lay priesthood in a way seldom found elsewhere since the New Testament period (though the most radical statements are in Luther and not in the Confessions). Do we wish to clericalize lay people or laicize clergy? Yet finally it is a conservative approach to ministry that, even in the passions of the Reformation, could keep bishops, if they let the gospel be heard.

13

Lacunae

David P. Daniel

For more than two decades representatives of various Lutheran churches in the United States have been engaged in seven bilateral (including one trilateral) "conversations" with representatives of other Christian groups. These dialogues have promoted serious, wide-ranging theological analysis and have fostered more cordial ecclesial relationships among them. Thus they must be considered a positive achievement of the ecumenical movement, and the time and energy devoted to them has been justified.

For purposes of evaluation the dialogues can be divided into three groups. The first group, which produced the majority of published studies and statements, is comprised of those conversations conducted by Christian communities which emphasize the historic catholicity and theological continuity of the church. Among these the Lutheran–Roman Catholic dialogue has been the most extensive, producing seven volumes of theological studies. The Lutheran–Reformed and the Lutheran–Episcopal dialogues also have produced several volumes of studies. All of these "churchly" dialogues considered a broad range of theological issues and were conducted, in the eyes of some though certainly not all of the participants, in order to identify points of substantive agreement and, by developing statements of consensus or convergence, to make possible a mutual recognition of their ministries and sacramental fellowship or eucharistic sharing.

A second set of dialogues, more recently begun, is that between Lutherans and representatives of "nonchurchly" traditions—those emphasizing orthopraxis, whose liturgical and theological traditions do not emphasize the historic continuity and catholicity of the church—namely, Methodists, Baptists, and Conservative/Evangelicals. These "conversations" have been more limited in scope and have produced fewer publications or recommendations for specific action. The goal of these dialogues has been less concrete though no less specific than the goal of those held with representatives of the "churchly" traditions, namely, to correct stereotypes, increase mutual understanding, and to improve ecclesial attitudes and relationships, but not to achieve consensus or to prepare for possible mergers.

The third set of dialogues is that composed of the Lutheran–Orthodox dialogue and the Lutheran–Reformed–Orthodox trilateral discussions, which face significant challenges and difficulties and still must be considered primarily exploratory. While the officially stated goal, mandated by the Orthodox participants, is "full communion as full mutual recognition," the non-Latin heritage of Orthodox Christianity and the paucity of previous theological or ecclesiastical interaction necessitates an extended period of familiarization. Thus these encounters have not yet produced any substantial body of published studies and only a few reports have appeared. As a result, the Lutheran–Orthodox conversations will not be considered in examining the *lacunae* in the ecumenical dialogues.

Before identifying gaps in the discussions, it might be wise briefly to establish the broad areas of theological and ecclesiastical concerns discussed by the dialogue teams. The agendas of all of the dialogues have reflected the specific theological and ecclesial concerns aroused by the modern ecumenical movement as enunciated forcefully, if not always clearly, in the document of the World Council of Churches, *Baptism, Eucharist and Ministry*. Thus all of the dialogues discussed aspects of the doctrines of the church, its ministry, and the sacraments.

However, the three "churchly" dialogues have considered a broader range of issues more thoroughly and have discussed the sacrament of the Lord's Supper and the apostolicity of the public office of the ministry far more extensively than have those with representatives of the "nonchurchly" traditions. In addition, the "churchly" dialogue teams have identified many similarities in their theological conceptualizations, methodologies, dogmatic formulations, and ecclesial attitudes.

The conversations with Methodists, Baptists, and Conservative/Evangelicals, on the other hand, exhibit a greater divergence of emphases and attitudes. The Lutheran–Methodist dialogue has been the most limited in scope, focusing primarily on baptism, faith, episcopacy and the Christian life while the Lutheran–Conservative/Evangelical discussions added to their examination of baptism a study of church discipline and scriptural authority. Neither of these two, however, included substantive consideration of the Lord's Supper in their published reports. The Lutheran–Baptist conversation produced three common statements which dealt with conversion, faith, baptism, original sin, the theology of the child, church, and ministry.

In addition to the concerns enunciated in BEM, which provided the general agenda for the dialogues, the shape and particular emphases of each of the individual discussions was further "contextualized" by those particular issues which traditionally engendered theological debate and ecclesiastical tensions. This contextualization through examination of the salient features of the historical development and theological formulations of the participants was utilized, however, for different purposes. In the "nonchurchly" dialogues contextualization was employed instructionally and descriptively to clarify particular ecclesiastical and theological positions of the dialogue partners without specifically considering how closer formal ecclesial ties might be established. In the "churchly" dialogues, however, "contextualization" was employed programatically and therapeutically to establish those points at which theological divergence had previously occurred so that alternate avenues of theological conceptualization or formulation might be found which would not only indicate theological convergence or agreement but also make possible a formal expression of the thus identified "sufficient" unity through closer ecclesial, sacramental, and liturgical cooperation.

Thus the dialogues as a whole were conducted according to the agenda set by the ecumenical movement and individually were shaped by specific traditionally divisive theological issues.

This had two consequences. On the one hand, discussions of issues not directly related to the specific concerns of the ecumenical movement or which have not been divisive seldom occurred. Moreover, individual dialogues tended to be particularistic rather than holistic, concentrating on a limited number of theological *loci* of peculiar significance for the participants without considering positions being enunciated in dialogues with other communities. In addition, issues were addressed primarily in terms of and with the methodological and terminological tools of classical systematic theology. Little attention was devoted to contemporary pastoral concerns and challenges, structural and functional problems facing modern Christianity, or implications of modern linguistic and epistemological theories for the task of theology. As a result, significant *lacunae* can be identified in the dialogues both individually and collectively.

It is the purpose of the observations which follow to evoke an awareness of the theological issues not considered or only briefly or ambiguously examined in the dialogues. Certainly not all the gaps can be noted. Rather, the *lacunae* indicated are representative. Moreover, ambiguities in specific theological formulations or expressions, especially in the various joint statements issued, will not be examined *per se* nor will particular, specific doctrinal statements or constructs be reviewed. Rather, the dialogues as a unit will be reviewed horizontally rather than vertically so that only those *lacunae* which can be observed in the discussions of theological or ecclesiastical issues considered by most or all of the dialogue teams will be noted. Finally, since the threefold concerns of BEM structured the dialogues, these categories will be utilized to indicate the major *lacunae*.

A. Baptism

While the doctrine of baptism was not discussed formally in the Lutheran–Reformed dialogues and only briefly treated during the course of the Lutheran–Episcopal conversations, it was discussed in the other dialogues. Many theological issues were considered, including original sin, the condition of unbaptized children, faith and the child, redemption and regeneration, and the initiatory and didactic nature of the sacrament, or, as the Baptists prefer, the ordinance. But in discussing the nature of the sacrament and when it should be administered, the question of the power of baptism to engender faith and the nature of that baptismal faith, so crucial to Lutheran theology, was not confronted. Nor were specific pastoral implications of the doctrine for modern moral problems, such as abortion and the "right to die," given much attention. As in most of the topics taken up in the dialogues, the consideration of baptism manifested a greater concern for dogmatic formulation than for pastoral implications and applications.

Likewise, the particularly vexing issues raised by the modern charismatic movement with its emphasis upon the so-called "baptism of the Spirit" or "Spirit-baptism" or "second baptism" were barely touched upon. This is more than a little surprising since the dialogues were conducted during the very decades when the charismatic movement and neo-Pentecostalism demonstrated considerable attraction and vitality.

Moreover, it is noteworthy that the Old Testament was not extensively employed to formulate theological positions or to identify doctrinal convergence. Yet contemporary theological concerns seem to require a consideration of the theology of the covenant and the typology of circumcision in the Old Testament in terms of its significance for the Lutheran view of baptism.

Thus, while Lutherans discovered a congruity of understanding concerning baptism with their "churchly" dialogue partners, they have also established that there are considerable differences between them and their "nonchurchly" discussants.

B. Eucharist

The doctrine of the sacrament of the Lord's Supper, the Holy Eucharist, or Holy Communion is for Lutherans a crucial theological *locus* since it has been the doctrine which has generated the greatest controversy among Christians. It is also the doctrine of major concern for those in the ecumenical movement who advocate eucharistic sharing or *communio in sacris* as both the sign and means of demonstrating ecclesial solidarity. In addition, the crucial philosophical and christological implications of the doctrine directly influence the doctrines of the church, its ministry, and fellowship.

It is significant that this doctrine was extensively discussed only in the "churchly" dialogues. It was considered briefly in the Lutheran–Baptist conversations, very briefly in the Lutheran–Methodist conversations (and did not appear in the published report), and was not treated at all in the published report of the Lutheran–Conservative/Evangelical discussions.

In the dialogues which took up the question of the Eucharist, the nature and purpose of the sacrament, the real presence of Christ, worthy and unworthy reception, the sacrament as a sign and symbol of the body of Christ and its unity, and the consensus required for eucharistic sharing were discussed. However, many significant doctrinal, pastoral, and practical ecclesial issues were not taken up or extensively considered.

Most significant was the reluctance of the dialogue groups to wrestle with the philosophical and linguistic framework within which they formulated statements pertaining to sacramental theology. While it was possible to recognize a convergence of formulation and conceptionalization with regard to the reality of the presence of Christ in the Lord's Supper, the philosophical and linguistic conceptual context of these formulations seems to have been intentionally left ambiguous so that differences in philosophical attitudes towards reality and theological truth were left unvoiced and unexamined. But it is precisely these perceptions, conceptions, and attitudes which undergird the particular theology of each dialogue partner regarding the significance, effect, and function of the sacrament in the life of the church. Moreover, since Christian theology today must be enunciated in a world whose philosophical context is quite different from that within which it developed, contemporary theologians must wrestle with the implications of modern conceptions of reality and modern linguistic theory for the formulation of sacramental theology. But this did not occur.

Such unvoiced and unexamined linguistic and philosophical attitudes can be perceived in two admittedly minor but illuminating observations. First, when speaking about the sacrament or about the

salvific work of our Lord in general, there is an observable preference
for utilizing the official ascriptive "Christ" in place of the personal
nominative "Jesus," which seems to indicate there is a need to
discuss further the relationship between the person of Jesus and his
work as the Christ. Yet Christology was not significantly examined.
Second, different designations for the Sacrament of the Altar were
employed. In the Lutheran–Roman Catholic dialogue the preferred
term is "Eucharist," while in the Lutheran–Reformed dialogue the
term "Lord's Supper" is more frequently employed. The Lutheran–
Episcopal dialogue seems to use both interchangeably but tends,
when speaking of questions of church fellowship, to employ the
term "Eucharist" while, when speaking about the Supper as sacrament, the term "Lord's Supper" is frequently used. The term
"Holy Communion" is also used but not in as distinctive a manner
as the other two terms. These terms, however, were not carefully
defined even though they do have different connotations. While the
term "Eucharist" tends to emphasize the human activity of offering
up, the descriptive "Lord's Supper" emphasizes historical and memorial elements, the designation "Holy Communion" calls attention
to the vertical and horizontal elements of fellowship. In the discussion of the Sacrament, then, Lutherans seem to have tailored
their language to the specific concerns of their individual dialogue
partners.

In addition, the discussions on the Lord's Supper generally avoided
the question of the actual reception of the present Christ by the
unworthy, the *manducatio indignorum,* and its implications for pastoral and confessional responsibilities. This issue, considered distinctively Lutheran by orthodox Lutheran theologians, has crucial
pastoral implications in situations where eucharistic sharing across
confessional lines is envisioned or advocated. Likewise, the relationship between church discipline and the congregational setting
of the Sacrament of the Altar in situations where transconfessional
communio in sacris or eucharistic sharing might be practiced was
not considered. The dialogues did no more than touch upon in passing
the questions of congregational and pastoral discipline or the proper
function of excommunication. Likewise, the institutional implications of the Sacrament as both an affirmative human act and a
causative divine act which take place in Christ within a vertical

fellowship of forgiveness and the horizontal fellowship of confession were not confronted.

Finally, the biblical foundation for "the will to unity" which focuses upon eucharistic sharing as the most suitable, visible, salutory, and therapeutic manifestation of unity was stated rather than examined. Yet must not the question be asked: Is *communio in sacris* truly an evangelic imperative, the most effective and necessary temporal symbol and realization of that unity for which Jesus prayed in his high priestly prayer or to which St. Paul exhorted his fellow believers? If so, several fundamentally neuralgic questions need to be addressed. First, if there is indeed a necessity to demonstrate unity visibly both ritually and structurally, is there not also a corresponding necessity to define when such demonstrations of unity are not only inappropriate but actually destructive? What are the conditions which not only give rise to but actually mandate separation? These need to be discussed and defined with more candor and thoroughness than has been exhibited in the dialogues to date.

C. Church and Ministry

Closely intertwined with discussions of the sacraments were those dealing with the theology of the church and its ministry. A broad spectrum of theological concerns was examined, which resulted in general affirmations of the unity of the true church in Christ and of the necessity for the public office of the ministry, together with declarations of the "apostolicity" of the ministry in the respective Christian communities. In addition, the "churchly" dialogues sought means formally and mutually to recognize the apostolic validity of one another's ministries.

The essentially clerical focus in the discussions of the ministry left substantially undiscussed the relationship between the clergy and the laity in the church, especially at the local, congregational level, and questions of polity. But to speak of the church in the world as a witnessing, confessing, and nurturing community also requires a discussion of how such tasks are to be effectively carried out in visible, organized communities. But while the dialogues sought to formulate statements on the ministry which indicated theological convergence, the practical applications of such formulations were not established. If it is the evident intention of some of the dialogue participants to justify not merely pulpit sharing but the possibility for clergy of one tradition to be called or placed in congregations of another, why this is desirable or how it might occur needs to be addressed.

Moreover, if theology is the exposition and application of God's word to his people, the means by which the fullness of his word is to be identified and established in faith and practice likewise requires thorough discussion, especially since there is much disagreement among the various discussion team members as to how the truth of the word of God is established, maintained, and applied, not necessarily *in abstracto*, but certainly *in concreto*. Thus much more attention than heretofore must be devoted to how the church actually exists and functions in the world and to a consideration of questions of ecclesiastical polity and confessional allegiance.

While questions of polity might be *adiaphora*, they are significant. For instance, if there is to be eucharistic sharing or a mutual recognition of ministries, its impact upon relations between and the responsibilities of pastors and congregations of the same confessional tradition to those of other traditions as well as to the *una sancta* must be considered. By whom and how are doctrinal and ecclesiastical issues to be resolved and maintained? What would necessitate the breaking or terminating of confessional bonds? If unity within "reconciled diversity" is indeed "a necessity," is it also a necessity to delineate when diversity is not, cannot, and should not be reconciled? The dialogues did not consider when it is both legitimate and necessary for Christians to view themselves as *in statu confessionis*.

Likewise the dialogues did not examine in a systematic manner hermeneutical and theological methodology or establish common principles to be used to identify, interpret, and assert the authenticity and authority of Scripture. It is not sufficient to discuss the contiguity, continuity, or convergence of theological understanding or ecclesial practice. It is also necessary to determine truth, to corroborate and verify the content of theology. While Scripture and its authority certainly has been discussed in the dialogue process, hermeneutical and heuristic concerns did not receive sufficient attention.

Yet precisely these concerns have generated considerable controversy and discussion within Lutheranism and the communities of their dialogue partners as well as between them. As difficult and painful as they might be, these issues must be discussed by those who maintain that there must be a "will to unity."

It is also instructive and interesting to note, moreover, that exegetical studies have been far less numerous than traditional systematic presentations in the dialogue process. But are not such exegetical studies necessary if the dialogue partners are to understand not only what are the particular theological conclusions of each but also the method by which their conclusions are established and the authority upon which they rest?

Finally, while pastoral care—preaching, teaching, consoling, exercising discipline, properly administering the sacraments, and leading God's people in and fostering among them effective and meaningful worship—are essential functions of the ministry, specific principles of pastoral care or liturgical practice have been given scant consideration in the dialogue to date. But does not the resurgence of a concern for spirituality or devotionalism require that attention be given to the formal cultic aspects of Christian life, to private prayer and devotion, and to modern moral problems? While Lutherans may properly question the connotative aspects of the term spirituality or spiritual formation, the theological foundations of worship and cultic practices demand consideration dogmatically, ecclesiologically, and even psychologically.

Likewise, though the characteristics of Christian life and ethics have received some attention, some of the most crucial moral issues of the day concerning marriage, divorce, the family, sexual morality, abortion, and the implications of modern medical technology and practice were not considered in the dialogues even though they trouble all Christian communities and require solidarity in witness. So also economic, social, or political questions, including issues raised by liberation theology, questions of economic and social justice, business and labor ethics, just and unjust wars, and the relationship between civic and moral responsibility cannot be ignored. Christians are called not only to be evangelic lights to the world, but to be preservative salt and sanctifying leaven in the world. They cannot avoid considering these matters of significance for

Christians in many different lands with variegated cultures and vastly different political, social, and economic perceptions and experiences. If improved understanding and cordial relations between the various Christian communities are to be achieved by the dialogue process, these issues, which have often proved divisive to and among Christian churches, must be considered.

A discussion of these issues might require, moreover, that future dialogue teams include not merely professional theologians or ecclesiastical leaders but also laypeople and representatives of local congregations.

Finally, though other theological issues or specific *loci* not covered by the various dialogues or which were only rather ambiguously resolved could be noted, two concluding observations are necessary. First, the dialogue process has been most helpful in bringing the various participants to an awareness "that although at times we use the same words with different meanings, we also upon occasion have quite different ways of saying the same thing." The dialogue process has heightened the awareness that despite diversity of expression and conception, the various Christian communities engaged in the dialogues and conversations do seek to give witness to the gospel of Jesus Christ. Second, it must also be recognized, however, that despite convergence of experience, theological method, and language, there still are major substantive issues which need further discussion and resolution. Indeed, agreement in conception and expression has not yet been achieved in the fundamental questions which still create difficulties for relationships between Christian communities, the very questions which have for two millennia disturbed and divided Christianity, namely, how do Christians understand and bear witness to the person and salvific work of the Lord of the church, Jesus the Christ.

PART THREE

Ecumenism from the Point of View of Each Church Body

14

Ecumenism in the Association of Evangelical Lutheran Churches

Martin L. Kretzmann

The founding convention of the Association of Evangelical Lutheran Churches was held in Chicago, December 3–4, 1976. When it entered the Evangelical Lutheran Church in America on January 1, 1988, it was not quite a teenager. To understand how it reached the point where it could participate in this Lutheran venture in ecumenism, it is important that we look at the events which led up to the formation of the AELC.

After the Lutheran Church–Missouri Synod took action against the faculty of Concordia Seminary in St. Louis at its convention in the summer of 1973, the "moderate" supporters of the faculty organized as a protest movement under the name "Evangelical Lutherans in Mission" in August 1973. In its constitution ELIM listed the following objective: "To encourage and pursue the active expression of Christian faith in mission and service to the whole world, the whole church and the whole man." The wording of this objective was taken from the Mission Affirmations which had been adopted by the LCMS in convention in 1965 and formed the basis of ELIM's understanding of mission in the world. The ecclesiology of the Mission Affirmations holds that the church is primarily and essentially the body of Christ in the world, gathered through the work of the Holy Spirit into one fellowship, living under the lordship of its head whose Spirit guides the fellowship in its ongoing fulfillment of his ministry. The third Affirmation, under the heading, "The Church Is Christ's Mission to the Church," says the following:

> RESOLVED That we affirm that the church is Christ's mission to the church. In obedience to the church's head and in sanctified loyalty to his congregation and his church body, a Christian will be ready with good conscience both to witness and to listen to all Christians . . . and be it further
>
> RESOLVED That we affirm as Lutheran Christians that the Evangelical Lutheran Church is chiefly a confessional movement within the total body of Christ rather than a denomination emphasizing institutional barriers of separation. The Lutheran Christian uses the Lutheran Confessions for the primary purpose for which they were framed: to confess Christ and His Gospel boldly and lovingly to all Christians. While the Confessions seek to repel all attacks against the Gospel, they are not intended to be a kind of Berlin wall to stop communication with other Christians; and be it further
>
> RESOLVED That we affirm that by virtue of our unity with other Christians in the body of Christ, we should work together when it will edify Christ's body and advance His mission, refusing cooperation, however, on such occasions when it would deny God's Word; and be it finally
>
> RESOLVED That we affirm that because the church is Christ's mission to the church, Christians should speak the Word of God to one another as they nurture, edify and educate one another for Christian faith and life. . . .

In the following year, 1974, the ELIM Assembly adopted a resolution titled "Here We Stand," which said, among other matters:

> We commit ourselves to persist as a confessing movement trusting in the free grace of God in Jesus Christ, in whom we have forgiveness and by whose Spirit we are called to freedom in the Gospel (and)
> To declare and to demonstrate appropriately our oneness with all who, by the leading of God's Spirit confess Jesus as Lord and Savior, and renounce all additions, conditions, or contradictions to God's free grace in Him.

At its assembly in 1976 ELIM resolved to "joyfully and confidently reaffirm our commitment to be a confessing people of God in accord with our statement of 1974."

In its May 1975 issue of "Together in Mission," (the newsletter of the ELIM movement) which was sent to all the delegates at the LCMS convention at Anaheim in July 1975, the following statement was made:

> Christ has only one Church. It is made up of all who, by grace, trust the promises of God, and through the leading of His Spirit accept the promises He has made through the life, death and resurrection of His Son.
>
> Regardless of denominational labels, there is only one Christian Church. It is the body of our Lord Jesus Christ. In it we share one hope, one calling, one faith, and one baptism, as the one Father of us all is present in all.
>
> God intends that the Church's unity be evident to the world, so that the world may see in that beloved community a sign of the way God intended His family to live together. Thus, our life and work together in Christ are a part of the Church's proclamation. Divisions are a result of sin and are a judgment calling us to repentance. When we live and work together in the world we offer a visible witness to God's love alive in us. Christians cannot condone, let alone support, divisions in Christ's body, the Church. . . .
>
> Against every form of sectarianism and schism, ELIM affirms that unity is God's present gift to all who are baptized and recognize Jesus Christ as their Lord and Savior. We seek to exercise that unity in fellowship and mission.
>
> Within the larger Christian community Lutherans have chosen to identify with each other and share a distinctive understanding of the Holy Scriptures. We accept the catholic creeds together with the Lutheran Confessions as faithful witnesses to God's purpose and promise revealed in Scripture. . . .

In its 1976 Assembly ELIM passed the following resolution entitled "To Recognize the AELC as One of the Fruits of the Confession of ELIM."

> ELIM continues as a confessing movement committed to the proclamation of God's love in Christ Jesus. As part of the confessing movement ELIM has sponsored two assemblies which through a resolution format have expressed a beginning understanding of the church and its unity and mission to which the people of ELIM have committed themselves.

Resolution 75-1 and 2 affirmed that for some their confession will be carried out more effectively in an institution separate from the LCMS. The board of ELIM was directed to facilitate that movement into a new structure.

The Association of Evangelical Lutheran Churches is the result of that effort. The preliminary Constitution of the AELC, in particular its preamble, make it clear that the AELC is committed to the same confessions and the same understanding of the church and its mission as is ELIM. In fact, it is clear that many of its understandings are a product of our experience as a confessing movement.

Resolution:

1. That we rejoice over the emergence of the new Synods and the Association of Evangelical Lutheran Churches, recognizing them as fruits of God's work among us.

2. That we encourage congregations and individuals to consider seriously the Synods and the AELC as a valid and viable alternative through which to be united in mission and ministry.

3. That we pray God's richest blessings on the people and congregations of the AELC.

The majority of individuals and congregations who formed the AELC in its early years were involved in the conflict between conservatives and moderates in the Lutheran Church–Missouri Synod. For the most part they were engaged in types of mission and ministry that were at variance with some of the narrow and anti-ecumenical principles which had developed in the LCMS. It is understandable that the principles articulated in the early AELC documents reflected the experiences they had gone through in the LCMS.

In the deliberations and resolutions of ELIM and other gatherings of people involved in the controversy in the LCMS it is important to note that those who felt it necessary to leave the LCMS did not think of establishing another Lutheran denomination. They spoke of a "life raft," of an "interim association," which would allow them to fulfill their understanding of the church and its mission without the suppression and harassment they experienced in the LCMS while they worked toward new relationships with other Lutherans. Although they saw the importance of a minimal constitution for the new association, they felt that the usual wording of constitutions could not convey the reasons why they were forming the new association. To give this background they prepared a preamble to the Constitution and Bylaws of the Association of Evangelical Lutheran Churches. This was also to serve as a response to those who often asked the "moderates" for a clear statement of what they stood "for" in addition to the many matters in the then administration of the LCMS which they criticized.

This Preamble, after a brief introduction, has four sections: The Church and its Mission; Lutheranism; The Scriptures; and a statement titled "In Hope," which gives the reasons for establishing a new association of churches. The whole of the preamble reflects the thinking and the theology of the "Mission Affirmations" adopted by the Lutheran Church–Missouri Synod in convention in 1965 and accepted by the "moderates" as a valid Lutheran understanding of the nature of the church and its mission. The following paragraphs are quotations or summaries of the sections pertinent to the ecumenical stance of the AELC.

> We are persuaded that the Church's one foundation is our Lord Jesus Christ, proclaimed and celebrated in the Gospel. Upon him and him alone our faith rests. . . . There is but one Church, gathered by the Spirit through God's gracious call and promise in the life, death, resurrection and expected coming again of our Lord Jesus Christ. God intends that the Church's unity be manifested to the world, so that the world may see in that beloved community a sign of the future offered in promise to all people. . . . The divisions in Christ's body, the Church, are a scandal calling us to repentance and renewed effort toward making evident that unity which is God's gift to those who share one hope, one calling, one Lord, one faith, one baptism, one God and Father of us all.

This, of course, was directed to those who overemphasize the invisible unity of all believers and neglect our Lord's saying "that the world may believe."

Regarding the Lutheran church, the Preamble says:

> We understand Lutheranism to be a confessional movement within the one, holy, catholic and apostolic Church. We rejoice in the unity we share with all who are baptized and by the power of the Spirit confess Jesus as Lord. We cherish what is distinctively Lutheran in our heritage, namely the Lutheran Symbols which so clearly testify

that we are saved by grace through faith. We see that heritage as God's gift intended not to divide but to enrich the whole Body of Christ.

The truth of our distinctive witness is not so fragile that it needs to be protected by isolation from the rest of the Church, nor is our understanding so superior that it does not need the response of the larger Christian community.

Concern for doctrine and concern for unity must never be set against one another. In fact, it is our concern for doctrine that makes all the more imperative our concern for unity since the unity of the Church is part and parcel of the doctrine of God's grace in Christ. That Gospel is our very life and we cannot permit it to be compromised in any way.

Temptation is ever present to seek security in schism or a sense of rightness in isolation. In opposition to such a course, we commit ourselves to unity within the Lutheran family, and to the renewal of the Lutheran confessional witness within the whole of Christ's Church. It is in the spirit of that commitment that we approach the organization of a new church body, seeing it as a step toward the closer fellowship in the Church we so earnestly desire.

One of the crucial matters under dispute with the administration was the interpretation of Scripture. The Preamble makes a lengthy statement on this issue.

The final section of the Preamble is entitled "In Hope." It is quoted in full here. It helps us to understand somewhat the agony of those who felt they could no longer remain in the Lutheran Church–Missouri Synod and also be faithful to their understanding of Scripture and the Lutheran Confessions. It also helps us to understand the ecumenical stance of the AELC.

In Hope

We prayed that the conflict between us and other members of the Lutheran Church–Missouri Synod might, by the grace of God, be resolved. It was our desire to live and work in fellowship with them because we did not see our differences as necessitating either strife or division. We felt there was a mutual need for correction and encouragement; and we asked our brothers and sisters in the Missouri Synod not to fear the testing to which the Lord himself was putting us, nor the change he might be working for our own good.

It appears to us now that our prayer is to be answered in a different way. Those who have disagreed with our witness have by majority vote elevated their understanding of Scripture to the status of doctrine normative for the whole synod, thus going beyond those confessional writings to which we have all voluntarily subscribed. They have condemned as heretical and schismatic those who take issue with their understanding, thus creating suspicion and fear throughout the Synod and fostering heartbreaking dissension, which has not abated but only increased as the controversy wears on.

In this atmosphere we find neither joy for our mission nor peace in our ministry. We recognize and repent of our own shortcomings in this struggle, and we seek God's mercy for a new beginning and a better way. We have concluded that our commitment to the Gospel of Christ, the unity of the whole Church, and the support of suffering brothers and sisters necessitates our joining together in a new association. In following that conviction, we repeat our commitment to ultimate Lutheran unity and to the renewal of the Lutheran confessional witness within the Holy Christian Church.

It is our desire to be conservative in our fidelity to the faith once delivered and proclaimed from apostolic times to the present. We wish to be moderate in our behavior toward those whose views are not precisely the same as ours. We wish to be liberal in our eagerness to apply our faith to every circumstance of human need. And we wish finally to be radical in our unqualified obedience to the truth as God has given us to see the truth, for . . .

We are persuaded that neither death, nor life, nor angels, nor principalities, nor things present, nor things to come, nor powers, nor height, nor depth, nor anything else in all creation, will be able to separate us from the love of God in Christ Jesus our Lord.

(In this spirit the Constitution and Bylaws stand as an invitation to share together in the great mission of God to which we are all called.)

As mentioned earlier, the AELC was only a little over twelve years of age when it merged with the LCA and the ALC to form the Evangelical Lutheran Church in America. During these few years it had not taken any ecumenical actions on a national level. It had participated in the ecumenical dialogues which were conducted by the Division of Theological Studies of the Lutheran Council in the USA and had, according to reports from those dialogue meetings, on the whole shown a positive attitude toward an ecumenical stance. The conventions of the AELC had passed resolutions to join the Lutheran World Federation (and were subsequently admitted into the LWF) and to study membership in the World Council of Churches. On the local level, however, AELC congregations and pastors had participated in many ecumenical activities. It is a matter of historical record that at its 1978 convention the AELC adopted "A Call for Lutheran Union" which recognized the fact that the LCA and the ALC were already engaged in exploring levels of cooperation and institutional adjustments "to further developments in American Lutheranism, including organic union." The Call also stated:

> Unity is the gift of God through Christ. In order to be functional that unity must sooner or later be expressed in some form of organizational union through which our unity of faith, understanding and purpose will be manifest to the world. Union is the human expression of the unity which God has given.

The Call then quoted a statement issued by the participating bodies in LCUSA in 1970:

> We affirm that the demonstration of oneness in Christ is a more effective witness to Christ's oneness with man than separation;

> We affirm that unity of activity is a more compelling witness to Christ's singleness of purpose than disunity;

> We affirm that organizational oneness is a more effective testimony to His Church's mission than fragmentation.

To which we of the AELC add our conviction that Lutheran union is an important step to the realization of Christian unity.

The "Call for Lutheran Union" then included the following:

> Therefore, relying on God for strength and guidance, affirming oneness with all in the Lutheran family, and trusting that our Lord's mission will be enhanced by a united Lutheran witness, be it
>
> Resolved, that the Association of Evangelical Lutheran Churches (AELC) call upon all Lutheran church bodies in North America to join us in making a formal commitment to organic church union in a form in which Lutheran life and mission may be consolidated at all levels.

After the adoption of "A Call for Lutheran Union" AELC President William Kohn commented: "It is a beginning—an action of faith to make a reality of our hope."

In a study paper prepared in advance of the Founding Convention of the AELC in 1976 by the Reverend Richard J. Neuhaus, an ecumenical stance is called for, particularly in foreign mission situations:

> Then there is the matter of cooperating in mission with other Christians, whether they be Methodists, Roman Catholics, or other. Our Mission Affirmations reminds us: "The Evangelical Lutheran Church is chiefly a confessional movement within the total body of Christ rather than a denomination emphasizing barriers of separation." Some people say we can cooperate in "externals" such as social service, but that we cannot pray, or worship, or witness together. God, however, is distressingly careless about our nice denominational distinctions. And it is His mission. To be in mission is to join with God in sharing His life-giving love through Jesus Christ. . . . Wherever people are joined in commitment to God's mission we have not only the freedom but the imperative to celebrate our unity in the fullness of Christian life together. We are joined by God's initiative, not by convention resolutions prescribing with whom we are, and are not, in fellowship. Convention resolutions can only recognize the unity God has already established. When convention resolutions defy "the manifold and dynamic mission of God" they are made null and void—not by our decision but by His design.

At the Founding Convention of the AELC in December 1976, Dr. John Tietjen delivered a sermon entitled "A Clay Pot for the Lord" (2 Cor. 4:1-15); he said, among many other memorable things: "Because we have discovered through conflict and division the unity which is God's gift to the church, we have to act on the unity we share with fellow Christians. We have rediscovered the truth that the Evangelical Lutheran Church is primarily a confessional movement within the total body of Christ rather than a denomination emphasizing institutional walls of separation. As we act on the confessional unity we share with other Lutherans, together with them we need to determine how we can best share our faith with other Christians as we work with them in carrying out the one mission of the church."

That same convention in 1976 adopted two resolutions which have shaped the life and ministry of the AELC to the present and are indicative of the kind of theology and ecclesial thinking which the AELC brings to the ELCA.

The first of these resolutions is entitled:

To Declare Our Commitment to be a Church in Mission

Background

It is essential that all institutional expressions of the church have a clearly defined understanding of the mission to which God calls His people.

The Mission Affirmations (1965) are such an understanding of that mission.

By their affirmation that God Himself is the Author and Guarantor of the mission, the Mission Affirmations call us to a servant role in His plan for the world, even as they call us to boldness in trusting Him and His Spirit as He uses us in that plan.

By their reminder that the whole world, though under judgment, is the object and the arena of God's reconciling love in Jesus Christ, the Mission Affirmations call us to be active and involved in the world, open to reach and be reached by all, not prejudiced or parochial.

By their insistence that the very purpose and nature of Christ's Church is missionary, the Mission Affirmations challenge us to expend our lives and use our institutions for Christ-like witness and self-giving service.

By their witness to the Church as Christ's Body in the world, the Mission Affirmations call us away from triumphalism to a mission under the Cross, aware that we are sent, as He was sent, full of joy and hope.

Many of the insights of the Affirmations have come out of the mission which we have shared with fellow Lutherans in other parts of the world. We are grateful for these gifts of God. We commit ourselves to the service to which they call us.

Resolved

1. That we recognize and affirm the Mission Affirmations (1965) as a faithful and forthright exposition of the mission of God to which we are called.

2. That we urge all persons and organizations forming the AELC to study these Affirmations as they call the church to a servant role in today's world, not seeking success in our institutional life, but seeking life for the world by confrontation of evil and proclamation of the healing and saving activity of God.

3. That we recognize with special gratitude our fellowship with Lutheran Churches in other parts of the world, in whose life many of us have been involved.

4. That we covet their ministry to us and commit ourselves to participate in partnership with them in God's mission to the world.

The second resolution is entitled:

To Declare Our Commitment to Maintaining and Expressing the Unity of the Church

Background

We are committed to the unity of the Christian church, beyond the differences of confessional emphases and theological systems. We affirm the "ancient Christian Consensus" (*Book of Concord*) expressed in the Ecumenical Creeds. We acknowledge that the Evangelical Lutheran Church is chiefly a confessional movement within the total body of Christ rather than a denomination emphasizing institutional barriers of separation.

We are called upon to exhibit and practice more openly in altar and pulpit fellowship an already existing unity of faith and spirit among confessional Lutherans.

We look to consolidation of the Lutheran family in the hope that Lutherans together may contribute the wealth of our confessional heritage and the strength of the mission we derive from the Gospel to God's world of peoples and churches.

We are convinced that cooperation with other Lutheran churches gives each of the churches and all of their members opportunity to work in unity and strength rather then in competition and brokenness.

We should in faithfulness to the Gospel cooperate with all Christians in carrying on God's ministry to His world.

Resolved

1. That the Association of Evangelical Lutheran Churches (AELC) publicly declare its commitment to the active expression of Christian unity. Toward that end we will provide for and encourage participation in activities by which the unity of the faith may be advanced, cooperating with other Christian communities and fellowships where desirable and feasible in carrying on the mission of Christ's church.

2. That the AELC recognize, announce and celebrate full altar and pulpit fellowship with all with whom we share subscription to the

Scriptures and the confessions of the Evangelical Lutheran Church, and:

a. Declare ourselves in continuing fellowship with the Lutheran Church–Missouri Synod and express the hope that our brothers and sisters in that church body continue in fellowship with us;

b. Specifically by this resolution offer our hand in fellowship to The American Lutheran Church and the Lutheran Church in America in which church bodies sisters and brothers have expressly voiced their desire for altar and pulpit fellowship with the AELC and its members;

c. Extend our offer of fellowship to other Lutheran church bodies in this continent and throughout the world;

3. That the AELC commit itself to participation in all efforts toward consolidation of the Lutheran family;

4. That the AELC demonstrate its commitment to cooperative ministry with Lutherans by:

a. Applying for membership in the Lutheran Council in the U.S.A., the Board of Directors being instructed to implement this application;

b. Applying for membership in the Lutheran World Federation, the Board of Directors being instructed to implement this application;

c. Applying for participation in National Lutheran Campus Ministry, the Board of Directors being instructed to implement this application;

d. Utilizing the services of Lutheran World Relief in our efforts to relieve suffering throughout the world;

e. Establishing mutually supportive relationships with inter-Lutheran agencies and organizations which provide special focus on particular ministries.

5. That the AELC instruct the Board of Directors, in consultation with the Synods and the congregations, to study the matter of membership in the National Council of Churches of Christ in the U.S.A. and in the World Council of Churches for report and recommendation at the next convention, meanwhile providing for such relationships and participation as will further the Christian mission, and encouraging such relationships and participation on the part of Synods and congregations.

In that same convention Dr. C. Thomas Spitz, the Executive Secretary of the AELC, gave an address on the topic: "Some Ecumenical Imperatives and Considerations," which gave the biblical and confessional basis for the AELC's ecumenical actions.

15

Ecumenism and The American Lutheran Church

Edward D. Schneider

There is considerable justification for the claim that the ecumenical movement is the most distinctive feature of contemporary church history. Building on the missionary experiences of the Protestant churches in the nineteenth century and spurred by the ecumenical spirit of the Second Vatican Council, churches have discovered new imperatives for exploring the ecumenical challenges and opportunities offered by this unique moment in history.

The major Lutheran churches in this country, working cooperatively through the Division of Theological Studies of the Lutheran Council in the U.S.A. and/or the Lutheran World Federation, have made their own unique contribution to the ecumenical discussions of recent decades. This volume reviews and evaluates the bilateral dialogues between Lutherans and other theological traditions.

My assignment is to relate this review to the contributions of The American Lutheran Church during this period. I do so as a participant in the recent work of the Division of Theological Studies, but the opinions presented are personal and do not claim officially to represent those of The American Lutheran Church.

I. Living in an Ecumenical Era

The American Lutheran Church came into existence in 1960. Its life has coincided, therefore, with that period of time marked by the most intense ecumenical activity and discussion. The ALC has participated actively in these discussions through its membership in the Lutheran World Federation and the Lutheran Council in the U.S.A. Through dialogues with Roman Catholics, the Reformed, Episcopalians, Baptists, Eastern Orthodox, Methodists, and Conservative/Evangelicals, the ALC has become increasingly aware of the theological traditions and practices of these churches and groups of churches.

This theological discussion has been carried out with a keen awareness of Christ's prayer for his disciples, recorded in John 17, "that they may be one. . . . so that the world may believe." The ecumenical imperative has been understood in relation to the missionary imperative of the church.

An indication of the ecumenical spirit of The American Lutheran Church can be gleaned from a 1968 statement of guidelines and principles received and commended by the General Convention, a statement which built upon earlier statements of the church:

C. As guidelines for fraternal attitude toward, and possible cooperation with, other Christian churches, the American Lutheran Church affirms:

1. Our obligation to recognize that God is at work in and through other Christian churches.
2. Our obligation to determine the extent of our agreement with other churches in our understanding and interpretation of the Gospel, particularly in its application to contemporary life.
3. Our obligation to help one another as churches to make a united witness in proclaiming the Gospel of Jesus Christ to all men and nations.
4. Our obligation to cooperate with other Christian churches in works of love, in order to manifest the concern of God and of his people for the welfare of all men, such as the relief and eradication of human misery and injustice, the search for world peace, and the establishment of the rule of law in international affairs.[1]

With this commitment to the ecumenical enterprise, the ALC was an eager participant in ecumenical discussion.

II. The Emergence of a Critical Issue

The essays in this volume describe the results of these discussions. In one sense we are at the end of an era with the creation of the Evangelical Lutheran Church in America and the demise of the Lutheran Council in the U.S.A. In another sense we stand at a critical moment because of the very substantial progress made by these discussions over the last couple of decades. New relationships with churches have been forged as a consequence of these dialogues.

Various themes are traced by the essayists in this volume, themes which have been understood as significant, or critical, or even central by the dialogue participants. It is perhaps neither possible nor appropriate to rank the importance of these themes.

It does appear, however, that one issue has emerged as among the most intractable in some of the dialogues and as an issue for priority attention at this critical juncture in the history of the dialogues. This is the issue of the ministry: how it is understood and ordered. The understanding of ministry seems to have emerged, particularly with some of our partners in dialogue, as the critical issue at this stage of ecumenical discussion.

Among the points in contention on the ministry issue is the matter of historic succession in episcopal office. Two quotations from recent literature illustrate the issue. A study by the Lutheran Council in the U.S.A. on "The Historic Episcopate" concluded that "the Lutheran tradition holds that the historic succession of bishops is not essential for the office of the ministry."[2] The study went on to assert that "when the 'historic episcopate' faithfully proclaims the gospel and administers the sacraments, it may be accepted as a symbol of the church's unity and continuity throughout the centuries *provided that it is not viewed as a necessity for the validity of the church's ministry.*"[3]

The Committee on Doctrine of the National Council of Catholic Bishops, on the other hand, has recently asserted in their critique of Lutheran–Roman Catholic dialogues that "in Catholic doctrine apostolic succession in office (through the sacrament of episcopal ordination) is not simply important for the transmission of the deposit of faith, *but necessary.*"[4] The contrast between these statements illustrates at least one dimension of the issue.

For its part, The American Lutheran Church in its response to *Baptism, Eucharist and Ministry* has been critical of claims that a threefold ordering of ministry necessarily expresses or serves as a means for achieving church unity. It has claimed that continuity with the apostolic tradition bears no direct or necessary relationship to threefold forms of ministry.[5]

The issue of ministry, much less the matter of historic succession or threefold order, cannot, of course, be dealt with as an isolated or independent problem. It relates to one's understanding of the church and one's understanding of the church in relation to the gospel. Finally it pertains to a basic question for future ecumenical progress: Is consensus in the gospel adequate for church fellowship (CA 7), or must there be fellowship in one office?

It is indeed fortuitous that the emergence of this critical issue on the ecumenical scene coincides with the mandate of the Evangelical Lutheran Church in America to engage in a six-year study of ministry.

III. An Enduring Legacy

Lutheran involvement in ecumenical discussions has always lived with the tension between ecumenical openness and concern for confessional integrity. The concern for ecumenical openness has meant at its best a *genuine* openness to learning and growing and being enriched through an encounter with other traditions.

The concern for confessional integrity has meant an emphasis on the centrality of the word and proclamation, of justification by grace through faith, of the dynamics of sin and grace. It has underscored the notion that unity presupposes genuine agreement in the truth, that carefully crafted but ambiguous language which glosses over significant differences will never ultimately serve the cause of ecumenical progress.

Bishop Johannes Hanselmann, newly elected president of the Lutheran World Federation, has stated succinctly the perspective of most Lutheran participants in ecumenical dialogues. He said: "The more profiled my Lutheran theology, the more I can contribute to the ecumenical movement, especially the doctrines of justification, law and gospel, two kingdoms and the Lutheran concept of freedom."[6] Lutherans have exercised care for confessional commitments lest the gospel to which those commitments have witnessed be compromised in our eagerness to find agreement with other Christians with whom we long for closer ties of fellowship.

The American Lutheran Church has given official expression to the tension between ecumenical openness and confessional integrity in its statement entitled "Ecumenical Perspective and Guidelines." That statement declares: "We continue to honor the creative tension between confessional particularity and ecumenical universality. . . . We affirm . . . that being confessional is proper; becoming confessionalistic and narrow impedes appropriate ecumenical involvement. We likewise affirm that being ecumenical is proper; becoming ecumenicalistic and broad impedes appropriate confessional considerations."[7]

As Lutherans face the ecumenical opportunities and challenges of the years ahead, they will do well to have careful concern for both sides of this creative tension, for then genuine ecumenical progress can continue and we may discover new ways of expressing God's gift of unity.

16

Ecumenism in the Lutheran Church–Missouri Synod

John F. Johnson

Perhaps no other item on the agenda of American Lutheranism is as self-revealing as that of ecumenical dialogue. Martin Luther was not a sectarian and neither are his spiritual heirs. The genuine identity of Lutheranism as a confessing movement within the church catholic is especially displayed in its wide-ranging dialogues with other Christian communions.

Lutherans in the United States have now been involved in national-level, officially sponsored, bilateral conversations since 1963. Beginning with the first series of Lutheran–Reformed dialogues, Lutherans have expanded their efforts to include dialogue with Roman Catholics, Episcopalians, Methodists, Baptists, the Conservative/Evangelicals, and the Orthodox. All of these dialogues have sharpened the distinctive insights into the faith which Lutheranism can contribute to the whole body of Christ. They have also enhanced the contemporary Lutheran understanding of other traditions so that stereotypical inaccuracies need no longer pose as barriers to fruitful communication.

Participating fully in these ecumenical dialogues, and benefiting from them, has been the Lutheran Church–Missouri Synod. This participation is but one consequence of the Synod's long-standing commitment to the goal that all Christians "embrace and adhere to a single true religion and live together in unity and in one fellowship and church" (CA, Preface, 4; BC 25). However, the fact that LCMS dialogue participants have from time to time considered it important to adopt a minority report at the conclusion of a bilateral indicates a somewhat different view of ecumenism than that held by others within the Lutheran family.

The purpose of this essay is to summarize the understanding of ecumenism and church fellowship which has undergirded LCMS involvement in the various dialogues evaluated in this volume.

Particularly relevant to this task are two formal studies produced by the Synod's Commission on Theology and Church Relations (CTCR).

In 1974 a report of the CTCR was issued under the title, *A Lutheran Stance Toward Ecumenism*. It consisted of four parts. Part I dealt with the theological basis for ecumenism in the Scriptures and the Confessions; Part II set forth basic principles for Lutheran ecumenism; Part III addressed priorities for Lutheran ecumenical endeavors; and in Part IV the Commission commented on ecumenical activity at the synodical, district, congregational, and individual levels.

In large measure the six principles identified in Part II of the document have set the tone for the LCMS approach to ecumenical dialogue in the past decade:

A. Lutherans recognize and rejoice in their oneness with all Christians in the *Una Sancta* and regard this unity as the presupposition for continuing ecumenical endeavors throughout Christendom.

B. Lutherans deplore doctrinal disagreements, religious disputes, and dissensions among Christians and will not omit doing anything, in so far as God and conscience allow, that may serve the cause of Christian concord (CA Preface, 13; BC 26; FC SD 11:95; BC 632).

C. The concord that Lutherans desire and seek is confessional agreement among *all* Christians that extends to *all* the articles of faith revealed in the Sacred Scriptures and comprised in the Lutheran Symbols.

D. Lutherans seek agreement in all the articles of faith not only for the sake of uniformity itself, or solely on account of the obedience we owe to God's Word in all that it teaches, but by the light and the power of the Gospel they seek agreement in all the articles of faith chiefly in order that "the Gospel be preached in conformity with a pure understanding of it" (CA 7:2; BC 32).

E. Lutherans hold that until such confessional agreement is actualized not only by formal acceptance of doctrinal formulations but by faithful adherence to the true doctrine in the preaching and teaching of the church the basis for God-pleasing concord and fellowship among Christians does not yet exist.

F. Lutherans maintain that the concord we seek cannot be attained by ignoring doctrinal disagreements or by negotiating a compromise, but by exposing and refuting error and by confessing the truth.[1]

That the Synod sees these principles as consonant with the vigorous pursuit of dialogue opportunities is explicitly acknowledged. "The Synod will avail itself of all opportunities to engage in conversation with other Christians," says the study, "so long as this can be done without compromising our confessional position."[2]

In 1977 the Synod asked the CTCR to prepare a comprehensive study on the nature and implications of the concept of fellowship. The assignment was renewed in 1979 and led to the publication of such a report in 1981. This report has two parts.

Part I discusses the nature of fellowship according to Holy Scripture. The discussion is summarized in nine scriptural principles. The first three principles focus on "spiritual fellowship" with Christ. The church is already united spiritually; Christian unity is the spiritual bond that unites all believers to the Lord and thereby to each other.

The next three principles relate the confession of the apostolic faith to the nature of fellowship. "Faith in the heart (*fides qua*) continues to be saving faith as long as it has as its object the Scriptural Gospel of Jesus Christ. God therefore commands that the church teach and confess the faith (*fides quae*) as it has been recorded by the prophets and apostles in order that the body of Christ may be edified and extended."[3]

The last three theses take up the concept of fellowship in terms of external unity in the church. Fellowship in this sense is something to be sought and established. The report emphasizes that the church cannot have a "take it or leave it" attitude toward external unity (and, by implication, ecumenical dialogue). The pursuit of external unity is a scriptural mandate.

In the second part of its study the CTCR attempted to draw out the implications of the nature of fellowship for church body relationships today. The document notes that with the advent of "denominationalism" in the nineteenth century Lutherans applied their fellowship principles primarily through formal declarations of altar and pulpit fellowship, but that more recently other paradigms for achieving external unity have been championed.

Taking these two documents together *(A Lutheran Stance Toward Ecumenism* and *The Nature and Implications of the Concept of Fellowship)*, it can be said that the Missouri Synod brings to its perspective on ecumenism a distinctive outlook on two themes. The first theme is unity *of* and *in* the church; the second is fellowship.

The New Testament images of the church, as, for example, the body of Christ (Eph. 1:23); the mother of all believers (Gal. 4:26); the bride of Christ (John 3:29); and the people of Christ (Titus 2:14), reveal that it is constituted by faith. Indeed, the church can only be defined as those who are Christ's, linked to him intimately by faith. In other words, the church is a spiritual reality.

Lutheran confessional theology acknowledges and reflects this conception of the church. When the Augsburg Confession states in Art. 7, "For the true unity of the church it is enough to agree concerning the teaching of the Gospel and the administration of the sacraments," it is correlating unity with distinctively spiritual realities. The church is not described merely in terms of a sacral institution, a hierarchy, or a canon law. In contrast, the Confession stresses that the church is a communion of faith *(est autem ecclesia congregatio sanctorum)*. As explained in the Apology (7:31; BC 174):

> But the church is not so much a society of external matters and rites like other states, but it is above all a society of faith and the Holy Spirit in the heart. However, it has external marks so that it may be recognized, namely, the pure preaching of the Gospel and the administration of the sacraments in agreement with the Gospel of Christ. It is this church which alone is called the body of Christ.

When one views the church in this way, neither from its human administration and arrangements nor from its membership rolls but fundamentally from its head, Christ, then one must say that the unity of the church is given. It is given with faith in the gospel. The unity of the church (*unitas*) is a fact established through Christ and guaranteed in Christ as the Lord of the church. This inner unity Christians can neither establish nor safeguard; it is the inalienable gift of God to his church.

However, the spiritual unity of the church entails a dynamic which works toward an external unity. The spiritual unity becomes manifest, taking on expression and effectiveness. For, quoting the Apology again: "We are not dreaming about some Platonic republic . . . but we teach that this church actually exists, made up of true believers and righteous men scattered throughout the world" (Ap 7:20; BC 171). We may know that the church is present when the external marks or signs are present, these being the pure preaching of the gospel and the right administration of the sacraments in keeping with the gospel. These signs remain the infallible indications to Christians where the church of Christ will be found. All other signs of the existence of the church are at best ambiguous.

Since the unity of the church in its most proper sense is already given by Christ, human efforts for its realization and actualization in terms of external unity (*concordia*) are provided by these marks. As Ernst Kinder has written:

> In our ecumenical efforts to bring about the realization of the hidden unity of the church, we cannot carry on arbitrarily as we please, in order to bring about unity at any cost. . . . Rather, our efforts are to be bound by the criteria which are given to us by Christ from the reality of the church itself. We should not aim at church unity with any methods or at any cost, but rather in keeping with its institution and continual maintenance by Christ.[4]

That is to say, the criteria by which we can judge whether or not an empirical, external church unity is legitimate are those "organs by which Christ in the Holy Spirit creates His one church as His body, preserving, erecting, ruling, and keeping it alive."[5] The word and sacraments are the means by which the church has been brought into being, and thus they are the means by which it is preserved and extended throughout the world. Accordingly only such external unity as employs the means of grace in their essential purity serves the true unity, preservation, and extension of the church.

Directly arising from this observation is the specific meaning of agreement "in the purely taught Gospel and the rightly administered sacraments." Or, more specifically, what are the limits of the term "gospel," the force of the *satis est?* This becomes the critical question for Lutherans engaged in ecumenical dialogue.

The tradition of the Missouri Synod has consistently maintained that one must talk about agreement in the gospel in the broad sense, that the entire body of Christian teaching is meant, named gospel *a parte maiore*. A number of reasons for this interpretation are adduced.

In terms of the confessional writings themselves, for instance, the internal evidence clearly shows that by "gospel" is not meant the bare essentials of the gospel (the gospel in the strict or narrow sense). Several citations may clarify this contention. In Art. 4 of the Apology Melanchthon says, "The Gospel declares that all men are under sin and are worthy of eternal wrath and death" (4:62; BC 115). In Art. 12 he writes, "For the sum of the proclamation of the Gospel is to denounce sin, to offer the forgiveness of sins and righteousness for Christ's sake, to grant the Holy Spirit and eternal life, and to lead us as regenerated men to do good" (12:29; BC 185–86). In Art. 27 he asserts that the gospel deals not only with forgiveness of sins and justification but also is "about true penitence, about works that have the command of God" (27:54; BC 278).

However, there is a much more important reason for the conviction that the external unity of the church is to be based on agreement in "doctrine and in all its articles as well as in the right use of the holy sacraments" (FC Ep 10:7; BC 493). The gospel in the narrow sense (the "good news" of the life, death, and resurrection of Jesus Christ) is directly related to all other articles of faith. To return to the terminology of the 1974 CTCR document:

> The scope of ecumenical endeavors is nothing less than the attainment of full confessional unanimity throughout Christendom with respect to all the articles of faith. This is *not* to say that the Symbols require a prescribable amount of agreement for the mere sake of agreement itself, or even that they attempt by a legislative use of Scripture to *compel* agreement *only* on account of the *obedience* that Christians owe to the Word of God. But this *is* to say that for the Symbols all the articles of faith are so integrally related to the Gospel in the narrow

sense (FC SD, V, 27) that error in any article threatens a correct understanding of the Gospel.[6]

The gospel through which the Holy Spirit calls, gathers, and enlightens his church ultimately involves all articles of faith.

A second ingredient in Missouri's ecumenism which impacts the dialogues, especially in terms of their practical goals, has to do with models for external unity in the church. The 1981 report included a study of four such models.

The first model is that of conciliarity or conciliar fellowship. Advocates of conciliarity recognize that unity in the church requires a level of consensus, but this should not be understood as implying a need for agreement in a complete statement of faith. On the contrary, consensus can be confined to selected fundamental affirmations. This means that "the traditional expressions of our identity as confessions and communions" must be recognized as "timebound in their terms of reference and relevance."[7]

The CTCR notes that the conciliar fellowship model entails both positive and negative aspects. On the positive side, the attempt to pursue external unity is clearly one with which Lutherans, including Missouri, identify. However, the conciliar model seems not to take seriously either that unity of the church which is given with faith or external unity in the church which is constituted by agreement in Confession. "As a result," observes the report, "the advocates of this model frequently give the impression that Christians can actually effect the spiritual unity of the church through their own efforts toward organic union."[8]

A second model is labeled reconciled diversity. According to this model, perhaps the most popular on the ecumenical scene, differences in doctrine are no longer regarded as divisive of fellowship. This position acknowledges that the church of Christ is by definition a confessing church but that confession of Christ is "expressed incompletely in the different confessional identities of the world families of churches."[9] In other words, a variety of confessional heritages are legitimate insofar as the truth of the one faith explicates itself in a variety of expressions.

Reconciled diversity shares with conciliarity the same basic strengths and weaknesses with respect to Lutheran confessional principles of unity. Like conciliarity, reconciled diversity correctly emphasizes the unity in the church which believers seek. Moreover, reconciled diversity grants that certain elements of common Christian understanding are indispensable. But in the final analysis this model presupposes that external unity can be based on agreement in the gospel in the narrow sense while allowing disagreement in other scriptural doctrines. Unity does not require uniformity of *faith* and order.

Third, the CTCR study comments on selective fellowship as a model of external unity. There is a number of variations of this model but perhaps the most widely held is the one which sees selective fellowship "as a church body's decision to allow each of its local congregations to decide on whether or not to engage in altar and pulpit fellowship with a congregation of another church body on the basis of a repudiation of the false doctrine(s) officially held by the denomination to which it belongs."[10] One of the major difficulties with this model is its promotion of a radical congregationalism which estranges the fellowship of local congregations from church body fellowship.

Fourth, the report sets forth as a model the historic Lutheran declaration of altar and pulpit fellowship, noting:

> The Lutheran Church–Missouri Synod, in accordance with this historical Lutheran precedent, has consistently followed this model with respect to its official relationships with other church bodies. Desiring to avoid both sectarianism or separatism as well as syncretism or unionism, it has sought external unity in the church through the use of the model of ecclesiastical declarations of altar and pulpit fellowship based on agreement in doctrine and practice.[11]

While altar and pulpit fellowship declarations are not divinely mandated, they do seem to take into account what Scripture teaches concerning the nature of fellowship.[12]

Admittedly the foregoing discussion of ecumenism in the Lutheran Church–Missouri Synod is but a cursory one.[13] What has been attempted is the isolation of specific elements in Missouri's ecumenical approach which have prompted and guided its engagement in meaningful dialogue. In sum, these elements include:

1. The desire to discover and establish closer relationships among all believers in Christ. At its 1986 synodical convention the LCMS adopted a resolution "to continue efforts toward external unity."

While the resolution noted Missouri's dissent from the "interim sharing of the Eucharist" proposals resulting from dialogue with the Episcopalians and the Reformed, it does seek the blessing of God on all discussions devoted to achieving unity in the church and urges that the Synod continue its efforts to carry out doctrinal discussions with other churches.

2. The possibility of distinguishing spiritual unity in the body of Christ from external unity in the church. An inner, spiritual unity is given the church with faith in the gospel. It is not a human construct but a "true spiritual unity without which there can be no faith in the heart" (Ap 7:31; BC 174). However, the gift (*Gabe*) is also a responsibility (*Aufgabe*). External unity in the church is a goal to be prized. It is constituted by agreement in the purely taught gospel and the rightly administered sacraments, that is, in "doctrine and in all its articles" (FC Ep 10:5; BC 493).

3. The conviction that agreement in the Confession of the Apostolic faith is the prerequisite for church fellowship. Where there is church fellowship in the sense of external unity, there will be altar and pulpit fellowship. Eucharistic fellowship is realization of church fellowship.

Behind these formulations are views that the Lutheran Church–Missouri Synod shares with many of its dialogue partners: a feeling of grave concern for the existing state of disunity among church bodies; a belief that the way to external unity by way of doctrinal agreement is the effort to reach a common understanding of the faith we live by, an effort to mean the same thing when we speak about the gospel; and the comfort we have in knowing that no matter what one observes on the ecumenical scene, the proclamation of the gospel and the administration of the sacraments still accomplishes what God wills.

17

Ecumenism in the Lutheran Church in America

William G. Rusch

It is over thirteen years ago that the Division of Theological Studies of the Lutheran Council in the U.S.A. undertook a review of ecumenical dialogues where United States Lutherans participated on the national level.[1] In the intervening years much has happened ecumenically, and it is indeed time once again to survey what Lutherans achieved with other Christians in these theological conversations. The Division of Theological Studies was fulfilling one of its assigned roles for the member churches in the Lutheran Council when in 1985 and 1986 it sponsored two consultations on this subject. Now in this volume the results of these consultations and the impressions of several members of the study committee are available to a larger audience.

My assignment is to relate this review of dialogues undertaken by the Division of Theological Studies in 1986 to ecumenism as defined and understood within the Lutheran Church in America. It seems to me that this means first to see how the Lutheran Church in America has viewed ecumenism, especially in regard to the dialogues. Then some observations should be made about American Lutheran dialogue activity on the basis of the two consultations sponsored by the Division of Theological Studies in 1985 and 1986. I should stress that these observations in the second section of this article are personal in nature and in no way represent official opinions of the Lutheran Church in America.

I.

In 1982 the Lutheran Church in America adopted an official statement on ecumenism, *Ecumenism: A Lutheran Commitment.* This document with the constitution and bylaws of this church represents its most authoritative teaching on this subject.[2]

The preface of *Ecumenism: A Lutheran Commitment* states that the Lutheran Church in America seeks to foster Christian unity. "This unity is God's gift in the life of the Church under Christ and the Spirit. Ecumenism is the experience and ongoing task of expressing this unity." This is a clear articulation of ecumenical understanding on the part of this church.

The vision of the commitment is based on the Bible and the Lutheran Confessions as those texts are read in the light of modern scholarship. This view is developed and commented on in section 1 of *Ecumenism: A Lutheran Commitment.* It builds on material in the Constitution of the Lutheran Church in America, especially Article 4, section 2, and Article 5, section 1. In these articles it is stated that there is a commitment to more than Lutheran union, indeed a commitment as well to foster Christian unity. "Christian unity may be sought even while hoping for Lutheran unification."

Thus in section 2 the Lutheran Church in America, drawing on these biblical and confessional resources, describes itself as a manifestation of the church evangelical, catholic, and ecumenical. *Evangelical* means to be centered in the gospel. *Catholic* means to be centered in the apostolic faith and its creedal and doctrinal articulation. *Ecumenical* means to be centered in the oneness that comes from God given in Christ.

Section 3, a brief history of ecumenical involvements since 1962, gives an account of the dialogues that have taken place between that year and 1982.

In section 4 there is an affirmation of the dialogues. It is simple but direct: "Bilateral and multilateral dialogues are to be encouraged."

The final part of the statement, section 6, is a series of commitments. Here the Lutheran Church in America commits itself to receive and act with promptness on reports and recommendations which affect external relationships from national and international dialogues in which it takes part.

This official statement teaches that the Lutheran Church in America at its highest level of authority affirms its clear commitment not only to the ecumenical movement, but as a part of that movement to the various dialogues in which it shared partnership with other Lutheran churches and to official response to these dialogues. As a result of this commitment, it is only natural that in the Lutheran Church in America there be strong support for, and interest in, the recent evaluation conducted by the Division of Theological Studies of the Lutheran Council in the U.S.A.

For me, in the context of this ecumenical affirmation of the Lutheran Church in America, a number of interesting items about American Lutheran involvement in dialogues became clear when the materials from the two consultations were assembled.

II.

One obvious characteristic of Lutheran dialogue activity in the United States is the relatively large number of churches or traditions with which Lutherans have been in theological discussion—a total of seven. This situation, not true in many other parts of the world, has been caused by a number of factors.

There is the pluralism of Christian life in the United States, with the result that not only are many churches and traditions present, but they have sufficient resources, numbers, and interest to promote dialogue.

The interaction of American society means that members of different churches meet in society, business, leisure, and education. This interaction often causes a desire on the part of church members to have their churches settle disputes that appear to be rooted in ancient history and irrelevant to modern life. No doubt American optimism and impatience with history have been among the factors that at least indirectly have urged the churches to begin talking with each other to settle their past differences.

Most American churches are removed by culture, thought patterns, and geography from their Middle Eastern and European roots. This means for many a separation from where some of the sharpest divisions occurred. This new context can encourage dialogue but sometimes at the cost of forgetfulness of important history.

These factors have influenced American Lutherans, as well as other Christians in the United States, and help explain the extensive and intensive nature of American Lutheran dialogue activity.

In view of the size and divided nature of American Lutheranism itself, one must conclude that United States Lutheran dialogues have been not only extensive but fairly balanced among the major expressions of Christianity in this country. The first dialogue for American Lutherans was with churches of the Reformed tradition. With several breaks it continued from 1963 until 1983.[3]

About two years after the beginning of the Lutheran–Reformed dialogue, planning began to put in place a dialogue in the United States between Lutherans and Roman Catholics. This dialogue started in July of 1965 and has continued its work to the present time. It has published an impressive series of volumes, now totaling seven in number.[4] Over the years it has gained a reputation for the high quality of its scholarly work and a preeminence among bilateral conversations. This is no doubt due to the caliber of theologians who have been appointed to this dialogue and the importance that both Lutheran and Catholic churches have assigned to overcoming their painful division of the past. But it is extremely important to observe that this dialogue never became the exclusive preoccupation of American Lutheran bilateral activity.

Both initial dialogues for American Lutherans reflected a sustaining power. The Lutheran–Roman Catholic dialogue has continued without interruption. While the Lutheran–Reformed has had its breaks, it has been taken up repeatedly over about the same period of time. Seen together, these dialogues provide evidence of the strong commitment of American Lutheranism to heal both divisions of the sixteenth century: the one with Catholicism and the other with the Reformed tradition.

After these beginnings of dialogue in the 1960s, Lutherans in the United States soon expanded their conversations with other churches or traditions. The latest evaluation by the Division of Theological

Studies of the Lutheran Council reveals this very clearly. A quick overview in alphabetical order indicates the range of American Lutheran dialogue activity. Lutherans have been in dialogue with Baptists,[5] Conservative/Evangelicals,[6] Episcopalians,[7] Methodists,[8] and the Orthodox.[9] Of this number the following are ongoing as of January 1, 1988: the dialogues with the Episcopalians, the Orthodox, and the Roman Catholics. Probably theological conversations will be resumed shortly with the Methodists and the Reformed.

Another significant feature of these dialogues is the varying levels of maturity. These dialogues are at different stages. The most developed is clearly the Lutheran–Roman Catholic dialogue, followed by the Lutheran–Episcopal and Lutheran–Reformed dialogues. All three dialogues have had official responses from some of the sponsoring churches to at least some of their work.

Two of these dialogues have been the basis for American Lutheran churches to enter into new relations with their dialogue partners.[10]

The fact that the dialogues are at different stages is understandable when a number of factors is kept in mind. Some dialogues have had much less time to develop; they simply have not existed as long as some others. The sponsoring churches have not been able to place the same amount of resources in each dialogue either in personnel or funds for meetings. The mandates of the dialogues have varied considerably. Also the number and nature of the church-dividing issues are very different. Then too there is the history of the relationships between the various dialoguing churches. For example, Lutheran churches in the United States have had frequent contact with and knowledge of other churches arising from the sixteenth century Reformation experience. There has been less relationship with the Roman Catholic Church, and it at times has been polemic. Lutheran and Orthodox churches until most recently have lived in isolation from each other. Thus it is not strange that the dialogues are at different stages of their work. It is much more important that they are in a responsible way addressing issues that divide the churches.

Because American Lutheranism itself is divided into several churches, the Lutheran churches that have entered into dialogue have sought wherever possible to carry on this dialogue on a broad, pan-Lutheran basis. This means that from the beginnings of Lutheran dialogue activity, The American Lutheran Church, the Lutheran Church in America, the Lutheran Church–Missouri Synod, and the Association of Evangelical Lutheran Churches (shortly after its establishment in 1976), were the Lutheran churches that other American churches encountered in dialogue.[11]

There are some obvious advantages to this arrangement. The Lutheran side is as representative of American Lutheranism as is possible at this time. Costs are saved for all dialogue participants. Lutherans are given the opportunity among themselves to grow closer together. This common dialogue experience was probably one of the factors that aided the three churches to proceed toward their merger in 1987.

On the other hand, disadvantages have appeared that cannot be ignored. Especially in recent years minority reports have become a feature of the dialogues. The Lutheran–Roman Catholic dialogue has been able to avoid this practice, but virtually every other series of dialogue has seen the Lutheran Church–Missouri synod's participants dissent from the majority report of the other Lutherans. How much this practice has impeded the progress of the dialogues is difficult to determine. It has shown some of the serious disagreements within American Lutheranism and raised the question of whether or not there is among American Lutherans a common basis and understanding for dialogue together. This question becomes even more significant as some Lutherans are finding it possible to enter into levels of fellowship with other churches, but the members of the Lutheran Church–Missouri Synod do not seem to be able to consider such an eventuality.

This essay has provided some reflection on the dialogues between Lutherans and other Christians in the United States by one member of the study committee of the Division of Theological Studies. A fuller account would require more space than is available here. Yet even from this limited presentation it is possible to see at work the deep commitments to the ecumenical movement of several Lutheran and other churches. Such commitments are reflected in documents coming from the Lutheran Church in America, including the official statement on ecumenism and the responses to various dialogue reports.

Notes

Preface

1. New York: LCUSA, 1977. Cf. the study done at the same time: Robert J. Marshall, (Chairperson), *Ecumenical Relations of the Lutheran World Federation. Report of the Working Group on the Interrelations between the Various Bilateral Dialogues* (Geneva: LWF, 1977). Roman Catholic evaluation of their own dialogues may be found in: "The Bilateral Consultations Between the Roman Catholic Church in the United States and Other Christian Communions. A Theological Review and Critique by the Study Committee Commissioned by the Board of Directors of the Catholic Theological Society of America. Report of July 1972," *Proceedings of the Catholic Theological Society of America* 27 (1973) 180-232; "The Bilateral Consultations Between the Roman Catholic Church in the United States and Other Christian Communions (1972–1979). A Theological Review and Critique by the Study Committee Commissioned by the Board of Directors of the Catholic Theological Society of America. Report of June 1979," *Proceedings of the Catholic Theological Society of America* 34 (1979) 253-85; "Bishops' Committee for Ecumenical and Interreligious Affairs Evaluation of the U.S. Lutheran–Roman Catholic Dialogue," *Lutheran Quarterly* ns 1(1987) 125–69.
2. *Mailings on Mission and Evangelism* (Geneva: LWF, June, 1986) 1–26. An emphasis on mission is found in recent dialogues; cf. *Episcopacy: A Lutheran/United Methodist Common Statement to the Church* (Chicago: Office of Ecumenical Affairs, ELCA, 1988), ## 7, 10; *Implications of the Gospel*. Lutheran–Episcopal Dialogue, Series III (ed. W. A. Norgren and W. G. Rusch; Minneapolis: Augsburg; and Cincinnati: Forward Movement, 1988), #93, cf. ##93-113; Anglican–Lutheran International Continuation Committee, *The Niagara Report* (London: Anglican Consultative Council; and Geneva: LWF, 1988), ##15, 21-23, 26-28, 34, 40.
3. 8 pp.; liturgy is emphasized in *Implications of the Gospel*. Lutheran–Episcopal Dialogue, Series III (ed. W. A. Norgren and W. G. Rusch; Minneapolis: Augsburg; and Cincinnati: Forward Movement, 1988), ##43-50.
4. Cf. Robert Hale, "Ecumenism And Spirituality," *Ecumenical Trends* 13 (April 1984) 59-61.
5. Further resources: A. Birmelé, *Local Ecumenism. How Church Unity Is Seen and Practised by Congregations* (Geneva: WCC, 1984); Nils Ehrenström and

Günther Gassmann, *Confessions in Dialogue: A Survey of Bilateral Conversations among World Confessional Families, 1959–1974* (Faith and Order Paper No. 74; 3rd rev. ed. N. Ehrenström; Geneva: WCC, 1975); J. F. Puglisi and S. J. Voicu (eds.), *A Bibliography of Interchurch and Interconfessional Theological Dialogues* (Rome: Centro Pro Unione, 1984); Ruth Rouse and Stephen Charles Neill (eds.), *A History of the Ecumenical Movement*, Vol. 1, 1517–1948 (Geneva: WCC, 1987); Harold E. Fey (ed.), *A History of the Ecumenical Movement: The Ecumenical Advance*, Vol. 2, 1949–1968 (Geneva: WCC, 1987); *The Three Reports of the Forum on Bilateral Conversations* (Faith and Order Paper 107; Geneva: WCC, 1981); *Fourth Forum on Bilateral Conversations: Report* (Faith and Order 125; Geneva: WCC, 1985).

Introduction

1. Printed in: Eugene Skibbe, *Protestant Agreement on the Lord's Supper* (Minneapolis: Augsburg, 1968), pp. 90–93.
2. "The Report of the Exploratory Episcopal–Lutheran Dialogue in the U.S.A.," LED 1, pp. 20–23.
3. "Lutheran Church in America," *Churches respond to BEM* (Faith and Order Paper 129; ed. M. Thurian; Geneva: WCC, 1986), 1:34; "American Lutheran Church," *Churches respond to BEM* (Faith and Order Paper 132; ed. M. Thurian; Geneva: WCC, 1986), 2:81.
4. *Ecumenical Relations of the Lutheran World Federation: Report of the Working Group on the Interrelations between the Various Bilateral Dialogues* (Geneva: LWF, 1977), #91.
5. "The Eucharist: A Lutheran–Roman Catholic Statement," L–RC 3, pp. 196–97.
6. Robert W. Jenson, "Lutheran Conditions for Communion in Holy Things," LED 1, p. 131.
7. "Lutheran Reflections," L–RC 6, #21, p. 68, and note 144, p. 309.
8. Harding Meyer, "The LWF and its Role in the Ecumenical Movement," *Lutheran World* 20 (1973) 27. WARC = World Alliance of Reformed Churches.
9. Cited in LED 1, p. 34. Emphasis in the original.
10. See further: Joseph W. Baker, "The Petrine Office: Some Ecumenical Projections," L–RC 5, pp. 213–24; Joseph A. Burgess, (ed.), *In Search of Christian Unity. Basic Consensus/Basic Differences* (Minneapolis: Fortress, 1990); Harold Ditmanson, "A Response to the Fries-Rahner Proposal for Church Unity," *Lutheran Quarterly* ns 1 (1987) 373–89; Heinrich Fries and Karl Rahner, *Unity of the Churches. An Actual Possibility* (Philadelphia: Fortress; and New York/Ramsey, N.J.: Paulist, 1985); Günther Gassmann and Harding Meyer, *The Unity of the Church. Requirements and Structure* (LWF Report 15; Geneva: LWF, 1983), Institute for Ecumenical Research, Strasbourg, France, *Evangelical, 'Liberation' and Charismatic Movements: Their Problem and Significance Within Ecclesiological and Ecumenical Frameworks* (Studies; New York: Division of Theological Studies, LCUSA, n.d.); Roman Catholic/Lutheran Joint Commission, *Facing Unity. Models, Forms and Phases of Catholic–*

Lutheran Church Fellowship (Geneva: LWF, 1985); *What kind of unity?* (Faith and Order Paper 69; Geneva: WCC, 1974).
11. Carl Braaten, "Justification," see below, p. 97.
12. André Birmelé, *Le Salut en Jésus Christ dans les Dialogues Oecumeniques* (Paris: du Cerf, 1986), pp. 298–302.
13. Robert W. Bertram, " 'Faith Alone Justifies': Luther on Iustitia Fidei. Theses," L–RC 7, pp. 172–184.

1. Lutheran–Roman Catholic Dialogue

1. *Lutheran World* 19 (1972) 259–73; also, *Worship* 46 (1972) 326–51.
2. Full bibliography is to be found in L–RC 7, p. 316; the common statements for the seven series of Lutheran-Catholic Dialogues are printed together in *Building Unity* (ed. J. A. Burgess and J. Gros; Mahwah, N.J.: Paulist, 1989).
3. L–RC 2, p. 75; cf. p. 82.
4. Cf. L–RC 1, p. 21; 2, p. 76.
5. L–RC 3, pp. 195-96.
6. Cf. also L–RC 3, pp. 14-15.
7. *The Eucharist* (Geneva: LWF, 1980) #51, note 36 citing Ap 10:2 and L–RC 3, p. 195.
8. L–RC 6, Roman Catholic Reflections #19, 3.

2. Lutheran–Reformed Dialogue

1. Participants in the first series of discussions were the following: *Lutheran*: Conrad Bergendoff, Herbert J. A. Bouman, George W. Forell, Martin H. Franzmann, Martin J. Heinecken, William H. Narum, Warren A. Quanbeck, and Theodore G. Tappert; *alternates*: Paul M. Bretscher, Harold Ditmanson, William H. Lazareth, and Fred W. Meuser; *consultants*: Paul C. Empie, Virgil R. Westlund; *Reformed*: William Fennell, Howard G. Hageman, David Hay, George S. Hendry, John Leith, Henry Stob, Brad Thompson, and Cornelius Van Til; *alternates*: Robert C. Johnson, Joseph McLelland; *consultant*: James F. McCord.
2. The essays, summary, supplementary statements, and the final report were published in *Marburg Revisited* (ed. Paul C. Empie and James I. McCord; Minneapolis: Augsburg Publishing House, 1966). See the Preface.
3. Ibid., p. 37.
4. Ibid.
5. Ibid., p. 104.
6. Ibid.
7. Ibid., p. 152.
8. Ibid.
9. Ibid., p. 177.
10. Ibid., p. 37.
11. Ibid., p. 104.
12. Ibid., p. 152.

13. Ibid., p. 177.
14. Ibid., p. 191.
15. At its 1966 convention The American Lutheran Church referred the report of this series to its Committee on Inter-Church Relations. At its 1967 convention the Lutheran Church–Missouri Synod voiced appreciation that the conversations had proven fruitful, had manifested a measure of agreement upon the topics discussed, and had frankly recognized and discussed remaining differences. It requested its Commission on Theology and Church Relations in cooperation with other Lutherans to take whatever steps would be necessary for participation in further discussions on national and local levels.
16. Participants in the second series of dialogue were the following: *Lutheran*: Ralph A. Bohlmann, George W. Forell, William H. Lazareth, Howard W. Tepker, William H. Weiblen, and Walter R. Wietzke; *alternates*: James H. Burtness, Arnold E. Carlson, and Eugene F. Klug; *consultant*: Paul D. Opsahl; *Reformed*: John H. Leith, Daniel L. Migliore, Thomas D. Parker, Henry Stob, M. Eugene Osterhaven, and Roger Hazleton; *alternates*: Arthur C. Cochrane, Robert S. Paul; *consultant*: James I. McCord.
17. *An Invitation to Action: The Lutheran–Reformed Dialogue, Series III, 1981–1983* (ed. James E. Andrews and Joseph A. Burgess; Philadelphia: Fortress Press, 1984), p. 54.
18. Ibid., pp. 56–58.
19. Ibid., p. 57.
20. Ibid., p. 58.
21. Division of Theological Studies' Minutes, March 1980, p. 32.
22. Participants in the third series of dialogue were the following: *Lutheran*: Keith Bridston, George Dolak, Robert H. Fischer, Edward Perry, Karl Reko, Howard Tepker, Walter Wietzke; *DTS representative*: William Rusch; *staff*: Joseph Burgess; *Reformed*: E. Colin Baird, Jane D. Douglass, Paul Fries, Aurelia T. Fule, Frederich Herzog, Eugene March, Keith Nickle; *staff*: James E. Andrews.
23. Division of Theological Studies' Minutes, October 1980, Exhibit C.
24. IA, p. 16.
25. Ibid., p. 115.
26. Ibid., pp. 16, 22.
27. Ibid., p. 29.
28. Ibid.
29. Ibid., p. 113.
30. Ibid., p. 6.
31. Ibid., pp. 10, 17, 31.
32. Ibid., p. 113.
33. Ibid., p. 4.
34. Ibid., p. 123.
35. Ibid., p. 117.
36. Ibid., p. 116.
37. Ibid., p. 8.
38. *Lutheran and Presbyterian-Reformed Agreement 1986: A Study Guide* (Minneapolis: Office of the Presiding Bishop, 1987).
39. *The Lutheran*, September 17, 1986, p. 23.

40. *Convention Workbook: Reports and Overtures,* 1986, pp. 109–110.
41. Ibid., p. 55.
42. *Marburg Revisited,* p. 43.
43. IA, p. 58. Italics in text.
44. Ibid., pp. 2–6.

3. Lutheran–Episcopal Dialogue

1. *Lutheran–Episcopal Dialogue. A Progress Report* (Cincinnati: Forward Movement, 1972), p. 13.
2. LED 1, pp. 14–24.
3. LED 1, p. 21.
4. LED 1, pp. 23–24.
5. LED 1, pp. 145–63, Pullach Report ##17–91.
6. LED 1, p. 159; Pullach Report ##76–77.
7. *Lutheran–Episcopal Dialogue. Report and Recommendations.* The Report of the Lutheran–Episcopal Dialogue, Second Series, 1976–1980 (Cincinnati: Forward Movement, 1981), pp. 22–43; further historical background is to be found in William H. Petersen and Robert Goeser, *Traditions Transplanted: The Story of Anglican and Lutheran Churches in America* (Cincinnati: Forward Movement, 1981).
8. LED 2, pp. 18–19.
9. LED 2, pp. 57–59.
10. See, for example, *The Lutheran–Episcopal Agreement: Commentary and Guidelines* (New York: Division for World Mission and Ecumenism, LCA, 1983).
11. *Anglican–Lutheran Dialogue.* The Report of the Anglican–Lutheran European Regional Commission (London: SPCK, 1983), pp. 8–22.
12. Anglican–Lutheran International Continuation Committee, *The Niagara Report.* Report of the Anglican–Lutheran Consultation on Episcopé (London: Anglican Consultative Council; and Geneva: LWF, 1988), p. 56.
13. Ibid., pp. 57–59.
14. Cf. ibid., p. 40, #81.
15. Ibid., pp. 41–44, ##89–96.
16. *Implications of the Gospel,* Lutheran–Episcopal Dialogue, Series III (ed. W. A. Norgren and W. G. Rusch; Minneapolis: Augsburg; and Cincinnati: Forward Movement, 1988).
17. Ibid., pp. 91–92, ##126–27.
18. Ibid., p. 100.

4. Lutheran–Methodist Dialogue

1. "A Lutheran–United Methodist Statement on Baptism," *Perkins Journal* 34 (1981) 2–6.
2. *The Church: Community of Grace* (Geneva: LWF; and Lake Junaluska: World Methodist Council, 1984).

3. *Episcopacy: A Lutheran/United Methodist Common Statement to the Church* (Chicago: Office for Ecumenical Affairs, ELCA, 1988). A volume of supporting essays by the dialogue members is forthcoming.

5. Lutheran–Baptist Dialogue

1. See "Lutheran–Baptist Conversations," *American Baptist Quarterly* 1 (1982) 99.
2. One whole issue, entitled "Lutheran–Baptist Dialogue," of the *American Baptist Quarterly* was devoted to the publication of the materials from this dialogue: Volume 1, number 2, December 1982.
3. *Baptisten und Lutheraner im Gespräch. Schlussbericht eines offiziellen Gesprächs* (Texte aus der VELKD 17; Hannover: Lutherisches Kirchenamt der VELKD, 1981).
4. "Lutheran–Baptist Dialogue," *American Baptist Quarterly* 1 (1982) 104.
5. Ibid., p. 105.
6. LW 40:146.
7. "Lutheran–Baptist Dialogue," p. 107.
8. See the report in *Lutheran World Information* 25/81.
9. "Lutheran–Baptist Dialogue," p. 108.

6. Lutheran–Conservative/Evangelical Dialogue

1. Published as one complete number of *The Covenant Quarterly,* Volume 41, Number 3, August 1983, with the title, "Lutheran–Conservative Evangelical Dialogue."
2. Ibid., p. 7.
3. Donald Bloesch, *The Future of Evangelical Christianity* (Garden City, N.J.: Doubleday, 1983), p. 17.
4. Indianapolis: Bobbs-Merrill, 1970.

8. Justification

1. Martin Chemnitz, *Examination of the Council of Trent* (Parts 1 and 2; St. Louis: Concordia, 1971 and 1978).
2. Ibid., 1:467.
3. Ibid., p. 481.
4. Ibid., p. 482.
5. Reprinted in IA, pp. 43–44.
6. Ibid., p. 44.
7. Ibid., p. 10.
8. "A Lutheran–United Methodist Statement On Baptism," *Perkins Journal* 34 (1981) 2, #2.
9. Klaus Penzel, "A Response to E. Dale Dunlap," *Perkins Journal* 34 (1981) 17–18.

10. "Lutheran-Conservative Evangelical Dialogue," *The Covenant Quarterly* 41 (1983) 7.
11. Chemnitz, 1:514.
12. "A Statement Addressed to Lutherans by the Lutheran Participants," LED 1, pp. 29–37.
13. "A Statement Addressed to Episcopalians," LED 1, pp. 38–46.
14. Ibid., p. 43.
15. LED 2, pp. 23–24.
16. "Lutheran–Baptist Dialogue," *American Baptist Quarterly* 1 (1982) 103.
17. Ibid.
18. Ibid.
19. Minutes, Division of Theological Studies, LCUSA, 3/17–18/76, Exhibit B.
20. L–RC 7, #164.
21. L–RC 7, #121.
22. L–RC 7, #94.
23. Carl J. Peter, "The Decree on Justification in the Council of Trent," L–RC 7, p. 225.

9. Baptism

1. Karl Barth, *Die kirchliche Lehre von der Taufe* (Theologische Studien 14; Zurich: EVZ, 1943).
2. Karl Barth, *Die kirchliche Dogmatik 4, 4 (Zurich: EVZ, 1967).*
3. Jürgen Moltmann, *Kirche in der Kraft des Geistes* (Munich: Kaiser, 1975).
4. Robert Jenson, *Visible Words* (Philadelphia: Fortress, 1978).
5. Raymond Brown and Krister Stendahl on the New Testament and baptism, Arthur Carl Piepkorn on the Lutheran confessional teachings, and Godfrey Diekman on Trent.
6. L–RC 2, p. 85.
7. Quanbeck, in L–RC 2, p. 74.
8. Ibid., p. 72.
9. Ibid., pp. 74-75.
10. *Perkins Journal* 34 (1981) contains the statement and the accompanying papers.
11. "We also share the biblical Reformation doctrine of justification by grace through faith. We are agreed that we are justified by the grace of God for Christ's sake, through faith alone and not by the works demanded of us by God's law" (#2).
12. There is another important discussion of baptism in the International Lutheran–Methodist Statement, *The Church: Community of Grace* (Geneva: LWF; Lake Junaluska: World Methodist Council, 1984). It contains an illuminating statement of differences on original sin and on the nature of church membership bestowed by baptism. See sections 50–51, pp. 19–20.
13. *American Baptist Quarterly* 1 (1982) 103. See the first statement, section 1.
14. First statement, section 3, ibid., 105.
15. Second statement, section 2, ibid., 107.
16. There are also important papers concerning baptism between very divergent traditions in the report of the Lutheran–Conservative/Evangelical Dialogue.

This can be found in *The Covenant Quarterly* 41 (1983). The brief common statement acknowledges "the importance of baptism" for both traditions, but the differences expressed in the supporting essays are very great.

17. BEM, "Baptism," section 4.
18. BEM, B, section 3; section 8.
19. Section 9.
20. Section 10.
21. Commentary 21b.
22. Both documents are available from the Office for Ecumenical Affairs of the ELCA.
23. *In Christ—Hope for the World*. Official Proceedings of the Seventh Assembly of the Lutheran World Federation, 1984 (LWF Report No. 19/20; Geneva: LWF; 1984), p. 211.
24. *The COCU Consensus. In Quest of a Church of Christ Uniting* (ed. G. F. Moede; Princeton, N.J.: COCU, 1984), 4:9a, p. 25.

10. Eucharist

1. LED 1, pp. 16–17.
2. LED 1, p. 157.
3. LED 2, pp. 25–29.
4. John Reumann, *The Supper of the Lord* (Philadelphia: Fortress, 1985), p. 195.
5. *Facing Unity* (Geneva: LWF, 1985), pp. 38–39, #76. Emphasis in text.
6. L–RC 3, p. 188.
7. Ibid., p. 189.
8. Ibid., p. 189. Emphasis added.
9. Ibid., pp. 190–91.
10. Ibid., pp. 191–96.
11. Ibid., p. 197.
12. Ibid., pp. 45–74.
13. IA Lord's Supper 4.1, p. 16.
14. Reprinted in Eugene Skibbe, *Protestant Agreement on the Lord's Supper* (Minneapolis: Augsburg, 1968), pp. 90–93.
15. IA, pp. 42–43.
16. IA, p. 68.
17. IA, p. 69.
18. IA, p. 19.
19. IA Lord's Supper 1.1, p. 14.
20. IA Lord's Supper 3.1, p. 15.
21. IA Lord's Supper 4., p. 16.
22. IA Lord's Supper 5.2, p. 14.

11. Ministry

1. In what follows the paragraph number of the world-level dialogue document or report is cited. The world-level reports are available in: Harding Meyer and

Lukas Vischer, (eds.), *Growth in Agreement* (Ramsey: Paulist Press, 1984). Some of the basic analysis presented in *Ecumenical Relations of the Lutheran World Federation* (Geneva: LWF, 1977) is drawn upon in the discussion of world-level dialogues.

2. L–RC 4, pp. 7–22.
3. IA, pp. 24–28.
4. "A Lutheran–United Methodist statement on Baptism," *Perkins Journal* 34 (1981) 19, p. 5.
5. *Episcopacy: A Lutheran/United Methodist Common Statement to the Church* (Chicago: Office for Ecumenical Affairs, ELCA 1988), #15, pp. 8–9.
6. "Lutheran–Baptist Dialogue," *American Baptist Quarterly* 1 (1982) 109.
7. "Lutheran–Conservative/Evangelical Dialogue," *The Covenant Quarterly* 41 (1983) 7.
8. L–RC 4, p. 11, #14.
9. William A. Norgren, (ed.), *What Can We Share?* (Cincinnati: Forward Movement, 1985), p. 55.
10. Ibid., p. 57.
11. #73; emphasis in the text. Cf. L–RC 5, p. 22, #32: ". . . even the possibility and the desirability of the papal Ministry, renewed under the gospel and committed to Christian freedom, in a larger communion which would include the Lutheran churches."
12. IA, Ministry 9.4, 10, p. 31.
13. *Episcopacy: A Lutheran/United Methodist Common Statement to the Church* (Chicago: Office for Ecumenical Affairs, ELCA, 1988), #10, p. 10. Closely related is *The Historic Episcopate* (New York: Division of Theological Studies, 1986), produced by participants designated by Lutheran church body bishops/ presidents and a study committee of members selected from the division's standing committee.
14. Ibid., #11, p. 8.
15. Ibid., #17, p. 9.
16. Ibid., #21, p. 10.
17. Ibid., #37, p. 14.
18. L–RC 4, p. 22.
19. Ibid., p. 32.
20. Mary Tanner, "The Goal of Unity in Dialogues Involving Anglicans and Some Implications for the Work of ARCIC II," pp. 9–10. The importance of this fivefold proleptic ecclesiological model is underlined by the mere mention of the issue of the ordination of women. This crucial ecumenical issue would not be so noticeably absent from this discussion if theological dialogue to date had dealt simultaneously with all five elements of Mary Tanner's model.
21. *Facing Unity* (Geneva: LWF, 1985). In a section of the document entitled "Forms and Phases of Catholic–Lutheran Church Fellowship," specific practical designs for the preliminary forms of the joint exercise of episcope are proposed.

12. Eucharist and Ministry

1. Faith and Order Paper No. 111; Geneva: World Council of Churches, 1982.
2. John Reumann, *The Supper of the Lord: The New Testament, Ecumenical Dialogues, and Faith and Order on the Eucharist* (Philadelphia: Fortress, 1985). Since publication of this book I have had access to the Moorhouse Lectures given in 1975 by G. D. Kilpatrick of Oxford, published as *The Eucharist in Bible and Liturgy* (Cambridge: Cambridge University Press, 1983), and am happy to see how much accord there is on several crucial points. I had emphasized, for example, the Lord's Supper as "proclamation of the death of Jesus" (pp. 26–34) and expressed doubt that the difficult Greek word *anamnēsis*, "remembrance" (1 Cor. 11:24-25; Luke 22:19), means everything people have read into the notion of "re-presentation." Is there a parallelism between "proclaim the Lord's death" (11:26) and "keep on doing this that I may be remembered" (11:24-25)? Kilpatrick, an Anglican New Testament scholar known for his work in text criticism and philology but also an active churchman, argues that in the Greek Bible the verb form of *anamnēsis, anamnēskō*, means "tell" or "proclaim" (Exod. 23:13; Amos 6:10; Ps. 45:17 [46:18]; cf. 2 Cor. 7:14-15; 2 Tim. 1:6), therefore "Do this as often as you drink to proclaim me" (p. 16). Kilpatrick suggests the genuinely Pauline emphases on institution, Christ's death and resurrection, and second coming are perhaps present in the later, "tedious" Eucharistic Prayer of Hippolytus. Kilpatrick is *not* inclined to see the prayers in Didache 9. 1–4 and 10. 1–7 as designed for Eucharists, but rather for "an ordinary Christian meal" (pp. 17–20); cf. Reumann, *Supper,* pp. 8–10, 12, 16–17. Thus *anamnēsis* means proclamation of some specific saving acts. Note also (pp. 66–67) his strong emphasis, with Jeremias, that the Last Supper was not a sacrifice (against G. Dix) but the saying of a blessing.
3. J. D. G. Dunn, *Unity and Diversity in the New Testament* (Philadelphia: Westminster, 1977), pp. 103–23.
4. *The Fourth World Conference on Faith and Order: Montreal, 1963* (ed. P. C. Roger; London: SCM, 1964). See esp. Section II, par. 45 (p. 52), partially cited in BEM, p. ix.
5. *Lutheran World* 19 (1972) 259–73; *Worship* 46 (1972) 326–51.
6. In addition to Schweizer (cited below, n. 14) and Dunn (above, n. 3), there are recent surveys by A. Lemaire, "The Ministries in the New Testament," *Biblical Theology Bulletin* 3 (1973) 133–66; Jürgen Roloff, "Amt/Ämter/Amtsverständnis, IV, Im Neuen Testament," and "Apostel/Apostolat/Apostolizität," TRE 2 (1978) 509–33 and 3 (1978) 430–45; and W. G. Kümmel, "Das Urchristentum, II. Arbeiten zu Spezialproblemen, d. Ämter und Amtsverständnis," *Theologische Rundschau* 52 (1987) 111–54. In using the Scriptures, most modern writers seek, of course, to use it constructively, to sketch a doctrine (or doctrines) of the ministry. Is there another sense in which the scriptural material has the function of always offering a critique of our "organized ministry"?
7. As I have argued in *Jesus in the Church's Gospels* (Philadelphia: Fortress, 1968), pp. 279–86 on "the Servant," and esp. pp. 446–47 n. 101 on Luke 22:27, "one who serves."

8. It is an important step in understanding early Christian ecclesiology and ministry to grasp that the contemporary synagogue and not the temple (which was in the hands of those who opposed Jesus) was a key influence. One should not be misled by the somewhat romantic pictures in Acts of the temple still as a place of prayer and witnessing (2:46; 3:1), for Luke also knows a theology that saw the building of the temple as Israel's classic mistake (7:2–53, esp. 47–50). In emphasizing "elders" (*presbyteroi*, 11:30; 14:23; 15:2, 4, 6, 22, 23, etc.) Luke demonstrates a continuity with synagogue organization. But this was scarcely an influence in a "rabbinizing" direction whereby, as some have argued, the disciples were little more than "tape-recorders," transmitting Jesus' words intact. The great freedom, under the impact of the Spirit, along with a fidelity to Jesus' teachings, is what impresses one in the gospel tradition, as I have tried to show in *Jesus in the Church's Gospels,* pp. 91ff. This freedom is also to be seen in the way Paul, Pharisee that he had been, familiar with synagogues, adapts pragmatic, *ad hoc* solutions from the Gentile world for leadership in his mission churches; cf. Roloff, "Amt," TRE 2:518–22, esp. 520.

9. This brief paragraph could be expanded into a monograph, but the emphasis on variety is amply justified by the secondary studies referred to in n. 6 above. Roloff, "Amt," TRE 2:518–20, sees Paul's contribution primarily in the theological basics: his and other ministries were anchored christologically, with the gospel constitutive; they were ecclesiologically directed to build up the body of Christ and functionally coordinated with the manifestation of the Spirit. On Phil. 1:1 as a hendiadys, where *diakonoi* brings out the "service" aspect of the "inspectors" there, for the edification of the community (and to prevent the *episkopoi* from losing the humility crucial to all Christians), cf. A. Lemaire, *Les ministères aux origines de l'Église* (Lectio Divina 68; Paris, 1971), pp. 97–103, summarized in Jean-François Collange, *The Epistle of Saint Paul to the Philippians* (tr. A. W. Heathcote. London: Epworth, 1979), pp. 38–39.

10. See E. Schweizer (n. 14, below) and the literature in n. 6.

11. *Novum Testamentum* Supplements 12 (Leiden: Brill, 1966).

12. Subtitled, *A Sociological Exegesis of 1 Peter* (Philadelphia: Fortress, 1981); see pp. 169ff.

13. *The Community of the Beloved Disciple* (New York: Paulist, 1979). This analysis has developed since Brown's Anchor Bible volumes on John (1966, 1970) but can be seen in his AB 30 volume, *The Epistles of John* (Garden City, N.Y.: Doubleday, 1982).

14. Schweizer's *Church Order* appeared as Studies in Biblical Theology 32 (London: SCM, 1961). See Kümmel's quite recent survey cited in n. 6 above. Note, among Protestant authors, C. K. Barrett, *Church, Ministry and Sacraments in the New Testament* (Grand Rapids: Eerdmans, 1985). Paul J. Achtemeier's promising title, *The Quest for Unity in the New Testament Church: A Study in Paul and Acts* (Philadelphia: Fortress, 1987) does not touch on ministry or even rival views of apostleship. How complicated concepts of *apostoloi* were in the New Testament period can be seen in Roloff's TRE article, "Apostel," 3:433–43: we must reckon with Jerusalem, Antiochian, Pauline, Lucan, and other views.

15. E. Schillebeeckx, *Ministry: Leadership in the Community of Jesus Christ* (New York: Crossroad, 1981), and *The Church with a Human Face: A New and Expanded Theology of Ministry* (New York: Crossroad, 1985). The most important Catholic treatments, beside Lamaire (nn. 6 and 9, above), are Karl Kertelge, *Gemeinde und Amt im Neuen Testament* (Biblische Handbibliothek 10; Munich: Kösel-Verlag, 1972) and his collection of significant essays by previous scholars, *Das kirchliche Amt im Neuen Testament* (Wege der Forschung 189; Darmstadt: Wissenschaftliche Buchgesellschaft, 1977).

16. Subtitled *A Feminist Theological Reconstruction of Christian Origins* (New York: Crossroad, 1984). But see the review by Robert Kress, *Theological Studies* 45 (1984) 729–731.

17. New York: Paulist, 1983. The subtitle runs, *New Testament Cradles of Catholic Christianity.*

18. Ibid., p. 76.

19. So Bultmann; cf. H. Koester, *Introduction to the New Testament* (New York: de Gruyter, 1982) 2:284–85, where Ignatius is interpreted as more charismatic than institutional.

20. Walter Bauer, *Orthodoxy and Heresy in Earliest Christianity* (Philadelphia: Fortress, 1971).

21. William R. Schoedel, *Ignatius of Antioch* (Hermeneia; Philadelphia: Fortress, 1985)

22. Bernard Cooke, *Ministry to Word and Sacrament* (Philadelphia: Fortress, 1976).

23. In *The Supper of the Lord* (above, n. 2) attention has been called to how, from our early uncertainty about who "presided" at celebrations of the Lord's Supper in, e.g., Corinth, there developed a growing notion that only an ordained person could be in charge. When this intertwined with a view of thank-*offering* instead of simply thanksgiving (by prayer and praise) and a view of clergy as *priests* who in religions of the day regularly had the duty of offering something *to God*, the stage was set for changes in both the concept of the Lord's Supper and the position of the clergy. A minister became someone who offered the eucharistic sacrifice. It was against the Council of Trent's view of a minister as a "sacrificing priest" that the Lutheran Reformation especially protested. This relatedness of sacramental understanding and the concept of the ministry deserves further study, especially in a day when, from Lutheran praxis, it sometimes seems the one thing the ordained do that the unordained do not is to preside at the Eucharist. See Cooke, pp. 264–66, 357; Hans von Campenhausen, *Tradition and Life in the Church* (Philadelphia: Fortress, 1968), pp. 217–19.

24. Cf. *Supper,* p. 123.

25. The sequence in 10:14–15a, undergirded by Old Testament citations in 15b–17, runs logically, reversing Paul's order (which begins with believers calling upon God): messengers are sent (*apostellein*) (by God); they preach (*keryssein*) good news (*evangelizesthai*); people hear, and then believe, and so can call on the God in whom they have believed. In shorthand, "faith comes from what is heard" (v. 17). But at the heart of the sequences stands the preacher, sent by God. God's message (in Romans especially, justification, 10:3, 5–6, 10) leads to a believing community, but only through the proclaimers; hence CA's

sequence of God, Christ, message, messengers/ministry, response, church community. A missionary character of the office of preaching is here apparent.
26. Cf. Wilhelm Maurer, *Historical Commentary on the Augsburg Confession* (German, 2 vols., 1976 and 1978; tr. by H. George Anderson; Philadelphia: Fortress, 1986), esp. pp. 59–85 and 188–204. For an interpretation and ecumenical application, see Avery Dulles and George Lindbeck, "Bishops and the Ministry of the Gospel," *Confessing One Faith: A Joint Commentary on the Augsburg Confession by Lutheran and Catholic Theologians* (ed. and tr. G. W. Forrell and J. F. McCue; Minneapolis: Augsburg, 1982), pp. 148–72. See further, Robert Goeser, "The Historic Episcopate and the Lutheran Confessions," *Lutheran Quarterly* 1(1987) 214–32, for reasons why "one must call into question several premises of the article by Lindbeck and Dulles" (226) on hermeneutical as well as historical grounds (228–29).
27. I am raising with regard to the Confessions the issue posed in biblical studies by source analysis and "canonical criticism." Just as we can trace out prepauline elements in his letters or sources behind a gospel as distinct from later redaction, so we can do source analysis on the Augsburg Confession. But the argument noted in (§14) above may mistake temporal priority of the draft of one article with structure and emphasis of the finished (redacted) document. Just as in New Testament studies we cannot assume the intention of an earlier unit remains that of the author of the final document, so here. The analogy requires going further, not only to the "canonical" form of the finished document, the CA in this case, but also its further meaning when placed in a larger collection, the *Book of Concord*. Here the question becomes whether the CA in itself is dominant or must be interpreted in light of later discussions, as in the Formula of Concord, on questions where the CA did not prove definitive. My own view calls for affirming the CA as a finished document, but reflecting its historical circumstances, a Confession that is central to the whole *Book of Concord*, but subordinate to the biblical witness.
28. L–RC 4, pp. 227–82; reprinted, with editorial corrections in J. Reumann, *Ministries Examined: Laity, Clergy, Women, and Bishops in a Time of Change* (Minneapolis: Augsburg 1987), where the setting in the dialogue and some subsequent literature on the topic are presented.
29. Charles Lutz, (ed.), *Church Roots* (Minneapolis: Augsburg, 1985). The subtitle explains the contents: *Stories of Nine Immigrant Groups That Became the American Lutheran Church.*
30. James H. Pragman, *Traditions of Ministry* (St. Louis: Concordia, 1983).
31. An account of CNLC discussions on the ministry is sketched in *Ministries Examined* (see n. 28, above), chap. 5.
32. Nils Ehrenström and Günther Gassmann, *Confessions in Dialogue: A Survey of Bilateral Conversations among World Confessional Families, 1959–1974* (Faith and Order Paper No. 74, 3rd rev. ed. by N. Ehrenström; Geneva: World Council of Churches, 1975), pp. 182–94.
33. Pragman, pp. 154–55.
34. In Schlink's *The Coming Christ and the Coming Church* (Philadelphia: Fortress, 1968) pp. 186–233, esp. 186, 229–33. Schlink stresses "the apostolic succession of the [whole] Church and of each of its members" even over that of

the "pastoral ministry" and calls for openness to "free charisms" also (pp. 187–92, 231). Much of what he concludes for is based in the picture he has sketched of variety in the New Testament, where there is "no interest in the chain of laying-on of hands by Apostles on their fellow-workers and disciples" (p. 199), but there is an interest (2 Tim. 2:2) in "the transmission of pure doctrine." Episcopal laying-on of hands "is not the *sine qua non* of the apostolic succession of church and ministry" and "it did not prove to be the unfailing remedy securing the apostolicity of Church and dogma," e.g., in christological controversies. When Schlink adds it is "a *sign* for the apostolic succession of the ministries and the Church" and that we should welcome it "and if it is absent, it is right for us to work for its introduction," that is said within the context that "this '*signum*' must never be dissociated from the '*res*' which it signifies, in other words from the traditional teaching of the Apostles themselves" (p. 232). The Malta Report (§57) allows that Lutherans "can grant the importance of a special succession" if preeminence in *teaching* is recognized and that uninterrupted transmission of office is not viewed as a "guarantee of the continuity of the right proclamation of the gospel."

35. Just as it is often said in ecumenical statements that the ordained person is the symbol of church unity, so it is commonly assumed a bishop provides the ties to the church's universality. But in a day of wide travel and far-reaching contacts by others besides (more than?) bishops, the proposition is worth reexamining. Historically, one suspects, bishops have often been, of necessity, parochial, their outlook national, regional, or less, their record no more universal than many others in the church. Have the executive directors of global missions or university professors who travel widely become *de facto* the voices of universality? Given time and budget, various persons could fill this necessary function in the church.

36. See the essay by Daniel Martensen in this volume, pp. 127–29, for discussion of this subject in current dialogue.

37. Ibid., p. 132.

38. While more common in the New Testament in the sense of (divine) visitation, good or bad (Luke 19:44; 1 Peter 2:12), *episkopé* can mean the position of overseer (Acts 1:20, for Judas' successor) and the office of *episkopos* (1 Tim. 3:1). One suspects the ready agreement in dialogues on use of the term as "office of oversight" suggests episcopacy in a later, formal sense to some that it does not (and need not) to others. "Fullness" may suggest a lack or deficit in the one party if it is assumed any church tradition has possessed it all along.

39. L–RC 5.

40. Anglican–Roman Catholic International Commission, interim report, on "Church and Ministry," in the Venice Conversation of 1970, in *Theology* 74, 608 (Feb. 1971) 65. *The Final Report* (London: SPCK, 1982), pp. 76–77, 85–91, with the citation from 98.

41. Martensen, pp. 124–27.

42. See my essays, one of them part of the LCUSA study process, "What in Scripture Speaks to the Ordination of Women?" reprinted now in *Ministries Examined* (n. 28, above), chap. 2 (originally in *CTM* 44 [1973] 5–30), together with evaluation and updating on the discussion.

43. Martensen, p. 133–34.
44. See *Supper,* p. 79.

15. Ecumenism and The American Lutheran Church

1. *Reports and Actions of the Fourth General Convention of The American Lutheran Church* (1968), p. 650.
2. *The Historic Episcopate* (New York: LCUSA, 1986), p. 6.
3. Ibid., p. 7. Italics added.
4. Committee on Doctrine of the National Council of Catholic Bishops, "Lutheran–Roman Catholic Dialogues: Critique," *Lutheran Quarterly* 1 (1987) 129. Italics added.
5. *The Response of The American Lutheran Church to BAPTISM, EUCHARIST AND MINISTRY* (Minneapolis: Office of the Presiding Bishop, The ALC, 1985), pp. 6–7.
6. "Hanselmann Elected LWF President by Executive Committee," *LWI Monthly,* August 1987, p. 3.
7. *Ecumenical Perspective and Guidelines* (Minneapolis: Office of the Presiding Bishop, The ALC), pp. 13–14.

16. Ecumenism in the Lutheran Church–Missouri Synod

1. Commission on Theology and Church Relations, *A Lutheran Stance Toward Ecumenism* (St. Louis: CTCR, LCMS, 1974), p. 12. Emphasis in text.
2. Ibid., p. 14.
3. Commission on Theology and Church Relations, *The Nature and Implications of the Concept of Fellowship* (St. Louis: CTCR, LCMS, 1981), p. 14.
4. "Basic Considerations with Reference to Article VII of the Augsburg Confession," *The Unity of the Church* (ed. V. Vajta; Rock Island: Augustana, 1957), p. 64.
5. Ibid.
6. *A Lutheran Stance,* p. 10. Emphasis in text.
7. *The Nature,* p. 22.
8. Ibid., p. 24.
9. Ibid.
10. Ibid., p. 29.
11. Ibid., pp. 34–35.
12. Ibid., p. 37.
13. The CTCR does acknowledge that there is a tendency to associate altar and pulpit fellowship declarations with an "all or nothing" approach to inter-Christian relationships. This has in part prompted recent discussion of "levels of fellowship" in various synodical forums. The development of this idea may have significant implications for ecumenism in the LCMS.

17. Ecumenism in the Lutheran Church in America

1. *Lutherans in Ecumenical Dialogue: An Interpretive Guide* (Studies; New York: Lutheran Council in the U.S.A., 1977).
2. See *Ecumenism: A Lutheran Commitment*, adopted by the Eleventh Biennial Convention of the Lutheran Church in America, Louisville, Kentucky, September 3–10, 1982 (New York: Lutheran Church in America, 1983). The following references are to this document by section numbers.
3. The published material from this dialogue can be found in *Marburg Revisited* (ed. P. C. Empie and J. I. McCord; Minneapolis: Augsburg, 1966), and *An Invitation to Action* (ed. J. E. Andrews and J. A. Burgess; Philadelphia: Fortress, 1984).
4. The work of this dialogue has appeared in seven volumes, L–RC 1–7.
5. This material had been published as *Lutheran–Baptist Dialogue* (ed. J. A. Burgess and G. A. Iglehart; *The American Baptist* Quarterly [Barre, VT: American Baptist Historical Society] 1 [1982] 97–215).
6. This material is published as *Lutheran–Conservative/Evangelical Dialogue* (ed. J. A. Burgess and F. B. Nelson; *The Covenant Quarterly* [Chicago: North Park Seminary] 41 [1983] 1–99).
7. This material is published in two volumes, LED 1 and LED 2.
8. This material is published as "A Lutheran–United Methodist Statement on Baptism," *Perkins Journal* (Dallas: Southern Methodist University) 34 (1981) 1–56.
9. This dialogue has published no material to date. It will conclude its current series of discussions in 1989.
10. In 1982 The American Lutheran Church, the Association of Evangelical Lutheran Churches, and the Lutheran Church in America entered into the Lutheran–Episcopal Agreement with the Episcopal Church in the U.S.A.; see *Lutheran–Episcopal Agreement: Commentary and Guidelines* (New York: Division for World Mission and Ecumenism, Lutheran Church in America, 1983). In 1986 The American Lutheran Church and the Association of Evangelical Lutheran Churches entered into an agreement with the Presbyterian Church, U.S.A. and the Reformed Church in America; see *Lutheran–Reformed Agreement with Commentary* (Minneapolis: Office of the Presiding Bishop, The American Lutheran Church, 1987). In 1986 the Lutheran Church in America also made an official response to the Lutheran–Reformed dialogue, third series, but this response did not alter the external relations of the Lutheran Church in America to the same degree as the action by The American Lutheran Church and the Association of Evangelical Lutheran Churches; see *A Response to "An Invitation to Action"* (New York: Department for Ecumenical Relations, Lutheran Church in America, 1986). In 1988 a Lutheran–Reformed review committee began to prepare recommendations, to be ready in 1991, on further stages of relationships and theological dialogue.
11. The Latvian Evangelical Lutheran Church (LEBLA), a member of LCUSA since 1982, has had a representative on the current series of dialogues with the Orthodox.